RECEIVED

D0129056

RY

THE
KETO
HIGH FIBER DIET

THE
KETO
HIGH FIBER DIET

MORE THAN 60 HIGH-FIBER RECIPES
FOR THE ESSENTIAL LOW-CARB HIGH-FAT DIET

DR. THOMAS KURSCHEID

TILLER PRESS

New York London Toronto Sydney New Delhi

CONTENTS

Introduction   7

1 The Keto High-Fiber Approach

Why Low Carb?   10
The Best Low-Carb Foods for a Keto Diet   14
Low-Fat Diets: A Total Rethink   17
How a Keto Diet Works   18
Why High Fiber Is Important   20
Macronutrients & Micronutrients   24
The Benefits of the Keto High Fiber Diet   32
Why Ketosis?   34

2 The Two Phases of the Keto High Fiber Diet

Phase 1: Keto Boost   38
Phase 2: Stabilization   39
The Best High-Fiber Foods for a Keto Diet   42
Keeping on Track   44

3 The Recipes

Phase 1: Keto Boost   51
Phase 2: Stabilization   101

Recipe Index   156
General Index   158

Introduction by Dr. Thomas Kurscheid

Do you want to lose weight? Or just be more healthy? No desire to give up meat, eggs, or cheese? Or perhaps you're vegetarian? Maybe you're looking for quick weight-loss results without feeling hungry. Or do you want to simply eat nutritionally balanced foods that will have a positive influence on your long-term health? All of these wishes can be fulfilled with the Keto High Fiber Diet.

The Success of the Low-Carb Diet

Low-carb diets have been a topical issue for many years, and there is certainly no denying the success that they have had in reducing obesity. What's more, we now know that a low-carb approach is not just suitable for effective weight loss, it's also an excellent everyday diet for maintaining general health and preventing serious illnesses. I will be addressing these important issues in this book and describing the latest scientific studies.

The Keto Boost

While more and more people now see how effective a low-carb diet is, it's the keto approach that is set to revolutionize healthy weight-loss plans. Once a year, keeping insulin levels particularly low during a monthlong "keto boost" (where you consume less than 50g of carbohydrates per day) works for the same reasons that make fasting so valuable. After a few days the body goes into ketosis, swiftly burning off its own fat reserves to compensate for the lack of carbohydrates being consumed. The body is then supplied with energy more efficiently than ever, a phenomenon that is in fact utilized in sports to enhance performance at the highest level.

To obtain maximum health benefits, it has been shown that twenty-eight days is the ideal keto period, starting with two weeks on a strict keto regime (with a maximum of 25–30g of carbohydates per day), followed by two moderate keto weeks (with up to 50g of carbohydrates a day). By following the two phases of this Keto High Fiber Diet plan, you will find you lose weight quickly and effectively.

The High-Fiber Approach

The problem with most strict low-carb diets is that the gut and its precious inhabitants do not get the best nutrition. We now understand that this underappreciated organ has a significant impact on our health in many unexpected ways. What conventional low-carb diets fail to provide to the intestine is sufficient fiber. On the Keto High Fiber Diet there is a plentiful supply of fiber, which helps you feel satiated, while also aiding digestion without introducing carbohydrates. This fiber even feeds the slimming bacteria in your gut and boosts your immune system. All the recipes here have been formulated to be low in carbohydrates but high in fiber, and these meals are extremely delicious and surprisingly quick to prepare, as you will discover.

1

The Keto High-Fiber Approach

High-quality fats and proteins combined with lots of low-carb fiber are great for both weight loss and general health.

Why Low Carb?

The first thing I want to do in this book is offer a bit of guidance given the current bewildering array of dietary advice. As a registered nutritionist, I have been seeing for years how effective the low-carb approach is for patients at my clinic and how well this diet can be integrated into your everyday life. After my latest review of the scientific literature and research, I'm an even bigger low-carb fan than ever, and I follow these principles myself. Compared with most other diets, low carb will make you feel fitter, healthier, and slimmer in the long term. There is one key reason for this: it keeps your insulin levels low. This sole factor has numerous positive consequences for your body. Hunger pangs are no longer an issue, afternoon sleepiness vanishes, and energy levels remain constant throughout the day.

The work I've done with my patients has shown that weight loss is quantifiably easier to achieve on a low-carb diet because, after a few days in low-carb mode, fat cells open up to enable fat burning. But the longer-term effects are also extremely beneficial. In particular, there is a reduction in cardiovascular disease and also cancer rates when insulin levels are low, because insulin is a growth hormone not just for healthy cells but also for cancer cells. That's why a long-term, low-carb approach makes sense from a medical perspective, even when you aren't dieting.

The Importance of a Keto Phase

Adding a keto phase (less than 50g of carbohydrates per day for a period of one month) once a year is a reliable way of reaching an initial weight-loss goal or shedding excess pounds that may have been accumulated over the year. At the same time, your body undergoes a cleansing process, which protects the health even of people who are slim, and significantly lowers the risk of many illnesses.

During this time, with so few carbohydrates on offer, insulin levels will sink particularly low and remain stable. A wonderful and immensely important side effect is that hunger pangs diminish, which makes sticking to the regime much easier. At the same time, your immune system is helped to do its job, and any cancer cells that may develop in healthy individuals are tackled in the early stages. Your metabolism switches over to burning fat, and you will experience an incredible surge in energy—quite the opposite of many other dietary approaches. Nothing can supply the body with fuel more efficiently than access to its own fat deposits. Once this increased fat-burning state has been achieved, it can be maintained for as long as you wish through moderate carbohydrate consumption. Those who are heavily overweight may opt to extend the second, more moderate keto phase until they achieve their desired weight.

HIGH-FIBER KETO

With a standard diet, most of the body's energy requirements are met by carbohydrates. If we fail to consume sufficient carbohydrates, our energy supply will be empty after about seventy-two hours. When this happens, our metabolism switches its energy supply over to ketones, which it obtains from fatty acids. Energy is then generated (extremely efficiently, it should be said) from our own fat reserves. This metabolic state is described as ketogenic or ketosis. However, previous low-carb or ketogenic diets nearly always resulted in deficient fiber intake, with a detrimental impact on the gut, which is quite the opposite to the Keto High Fiber Diet. With this approach, high-quality fats and proteins combined with lots of low-carb fiber help promote intestinal detox processes and improve your gut health.

Looking Back

The Keto High Fiber Diet is the diet that suits most people best both genetically and physiologically. After all, for most of human history there was only limited availability of the carbohydrates we eat today, such as rice, potatoes, pasta, and bread. Carbohydrates were only introduced when humans settled in one place and began cultivating crops. Our bodies are therefore actually optimized for fat burning, as for most of our history the ketogenic diet was the only option available.

Alongside this, our cellular powerhouses, or mitochondria, function more effectively when on a high-fat, low-carbohydrate diet. This in turn produces fewer free radicals, the aggressive oxygen molecules that can damage our cells.

Ketogenic diet studies show not only that a keto approach is good for losing weight, it also keeps you healthy and can be beneficial for people suffering from serious illnesses, such as certain cancers. Keto isn't just suitable for short-term weight loss, it's also a sustainable long-term dietary option. With a regular twenty-eight-day keto phase, which I recommend once a year, you can trim down unwanted weight gain in a healthy manner. Meanwhile, your lower insulin levels will at the same time help

combat illnesses associated with excess weight, such as impairments to the liver. You will also get healthier results for your blood pressure, cholesterol, and blood sugar levels.

When humans were engaged in hard physical work such as farming, we burned off everything we ate, including carbohydrates. Thanks to today's largely sedentary lifestyles, this is no longer the case for most people, which has consequences for our health. This change has been accompanied by another sinister development: industrialized food production. Carbohydrates have become increasingly processed and concentrated: white rice, flour, and sugar are all calories in their purest form.

A Keto Phase and Fasting Have Similar Effects

When I recommend a low-carb diet or a keto phase to one of my patients, I'm often asked whether this offers adequate nutrition. My response is unequivocal: we can live exceptionally well with very few or no carbohydrates. We can indeed survive well for weeks without consuming any food provided we have enough to drink. This conscious abstinence from food is known as fasting and, if implemented regularly, has similarly beneficial effects to our health as are observed when people go completely without carbohydrates for a short period in a ketogenic diet.

GOOD HEALTH IS ABOUT MORE THAN NOT BEING SICK

Living a healthy life has many facets. On the one hand, there is physical health, which can be supported by adjusting our carbohydrate intake, eating a nutritious diet, and engaging in physical exercise. On the other hand, our mental health depends on the interplay between tension and relaxation, with a crucial contribution being made by inner contentment. A good diet impacts every area, including our immune system and its control center, our microbiome, which is not just vital for digestion but also affects our susceptibility to illness. A healthy diet also improves sleep and performance, and is a prerequisite for happiness.

The Best Low-Carb Foods for a Keto Diet

Some foods are inherently ketogenic, which means they have a keto factor (see page 43) of at least 70. These include fats, oils, high-fat varieties of cheese, black olives, coconut milk, almonds, and other nuts and seeds (flaxseed, sesame). Other foods, such as eggs and most kinds of meat and fish, are good because they contain few, if any, carbohydrates.

CHEESE	CARBS PER 100G
Brie	1g
Cheddar	0.5g
Feta	0g
Goat cheese	0.1g
Gouda	0g
Mozzarella	0g
Parmesan	0g
Roquefort	1.8g

DAIRY PRODUCTS	CARBS PER 100G
Buttermilk	4g
Cream cheese	2.6g
Cottage cheese	0g
Greek yogurt	4g
Mascarpone	3.6g
Milk	4.9g
Plain yogurt	4.1g
Sour cream	3.7g
Whipped cream	3.4g

FISH	CARBS PER 100G

Halibut, Herring, Cod, Caviar, Salmon, Smoked mackerel, Turbot, Tuna *(all 0g carbohydrates)*

SEAFOOD	CARBS PER 100G
Lobster	0g
Mussels	2.4g
Oysters	4.8g
Shrimp	0g
Squid	0g

EGGS	CARBS PER 100G
Eggs	0.7g
Egg yolk	0.3g

FAT/OIL	CARBS PER 100G
Clarified butter (ghee)	0g
Coconut milk (full-fat)	6g
Coconut oil (cold-pressed)	0g
Flaxseed oil	0g
Olive oil	0g
Peanut oil	0g
Pumpkin seed oil	0g
Wheatgerm oil	0g

NUTS & SEEDS	CARBS PER 100G
Almonds	5.4g
Almond butter	19.7g
Brazil nuts	3.6g
Coconut, ripe	4.8g
Hazelnuts	10.5g
Macadamia nuts	4g
Peanuts	7.5g
Pecans	4.4g
Pistachios	11.6g
Pumpkin seeds	14.2g
Sesame seeds	10.2g
Shredded coconut (unsweetened)	6.4g
Sunflower seeds	12.3g
Tahini (sesame)	6g
Walnuts	10.6g

In combination with fat, these can readily be classified as ketogenic foods. The same is true for the vegetables listed, which have less than 5g of carbohydrates per 100g. Once again, the important thing is to achieve a healthy combination with nuts, seeds, and oils. You will find ingredients that are particularly high in fiber and low in carbohydrates on pages 42 and 43.

MEAT	CARBS PER 100G
Duck, Chicken, Veal, Venison, Rabbit, Lamb, Beef, Pork *(all 0g carbohydrates)*	

VEGETABLES	CARBS PER 100G
Alfalfa	2.1g
Artichokes	2.6g
Arugula	2.1g
Asparagus	2g
Bamboo shoots	1g
Bean sprouts	2.3g
Beet leaves	2g
Broccoli	2.5g
Brussels sprouts	3.3g
Cauliflower	2.3g
Celery	2g
Celery root	2.3g
Chanterelles	0.2g
Chives	1.6g
Chicory	2.4g
Cucumber	1.8g
Daikon	2.4g
Eggplant	2.5g
Endive	1.2g
Fennel	2.8g
Iceberg lettuce	1.9g
Jerusalem artichoke	4g
Kale	2.5g
Kohlrabi	3.7g
Leek	3.3g
Mushrooms	0.6g
Napa cabbage	1.2g
Oyster mushrooms	0g
Swiss chard	0.7g
Pepper	2.9g
Parsnip	12.1g
Pumpkin (except Hokkaido)	4.6g
Radicchio	1.5g
Radishes	2.1g
Romaine lettuce	2g
Salsify	2.1g
Sauerkraut	0.8g
Spinach	0.6g
Tomatoes	2.6g
White cabbage	4.2g
Savoy	2.4g
Watercress	0.4g
Zucchini	2.2g

FRUIT	CARBS PER 100G
Avocado	0.4g
Lemon juice	2.4g
Olives, green	1.8g
Papaya, green	7.1g

MODERATELY KETO	CARBS PER 100G
Blackberries	6.2g
Blueberries	6.1g
Lime juice	8.4g
Raspberries	4.8g
Red currants	4.8g
Strawberries	5.5g

WHAT WE MEAN BY LOW CARB, KETO, AND HIGH FIBER

It's important to understand the terms that surround a ketogenic diet as ketosis can only be achieved by making sure that the recommended daily carbohydrate consumption is not exceeded.

A Normal Diet
A typical everyday diet has an average of 350g of carbohydrates per day. From a health perspective, this is far too high and is associated with significant long-term health risks.

A Ketogenic Diet
A ketogenic diet means that your daily carbohydrate consumption does not exceed 50g.

A Strictly Ketogenic Diet
A strictly ketogenic diet means less than 30g of carbohydrates per day.

On both ketogenic diets, at least 70 percent of calories consumed should consist of healthy fats (see page 24).

A Low-Carb Diet
A low-carb diet refers to an intake of 50 to 100g of carbohydrates per day. These should be high-quality carbohydrates, not highly processed ones, which the body can then metabolize slowly. Any diet in which there is a range of 100 to 150g of carbohydrates per day we refer to as a moderate low-carb regime.

A High-Fiber Diet
Almost all of us are consuming insufficient fiber. International recommendations for fiber intake are at least 25 to 30g per day, which I believe is still too low, even though most people fail to meet these targets. When we describe a high-fiber diet to promote optimal health and a healthy gut, this means a minimum intake of 35 to 40g of fiber per day.

Low-Fat Diets: A Total Rethink

Those of us who have been following this area for a while will still remember the hype surrounding cardiologist Robert Atkins, whose low-carb diet book was first published in the 1970s. Atkins's theory was that carbohydrates, rather than fat, were the primary cause of the increasing levels of obesity seen at that time. In a television interview with Larry King in 2003, Atkins argued for the elimination in particular of "refined carbohydrates"—in other words, industrially processed sugar and white flour, which lack fiber content. Both sugar and all-purpose flour are released quickly into the bloodstream, resulting in a rapid rise in insulin trying to trap sugar in the blood and transfer it into the body's cells. With complex carbohydrates, such as whole grains, vegetables, and beans, this process takes longer or is avoided completely.

Atkins faced considerable opposition from the experts of the time because his hypothesis contradicted the prevailing orthodoxy. Most doctors believed it was fundamentally unhealthy to go without carbohydrates, having been led astray by the *Seven Countries Study* by Ancel Keys, in which Keys claimed to show a clear connection between fat consumption and deaths caused by coronary artery disease. Unfortunately, these results proved to be bogus because he cherry-picked seven countries out of the twenty-two he studied and simply omitted those that did not fit his theory.

Sadly, most of Keys' scientific contemporaries and the 1970s US government were taken in. The result was an unprecedented fad for low-fat foods, which resulted in fats such as butter being completely discredited while sugar and other carbohydrates became increasingly popular. Once fat, with all its flavor-enhancing properties, was abandoned, a substitute was needed. So the proportion of sugar and carbohydrates in the average diet rose dramatically. Even now, forty years on, this low-fat mind-set is hard to shake off.

As I discussed earlier, before people engaged in agriculture, their carbohydrate consumption was very low. A successful hunt would primarily have involved meat with, at most, a few berries, some nuts, wild vegetables, and herbs found along the way. People performed extremely well on this diet—indeed, they had to in order to protect themselves against their enemies and to be able to hunt successfully. The Inuit people still predominantly eat this way today, and they are virtually immune to cardiovascular disease and tooth decay. So we should not in any way see a low-carbohydrate diet as some new dieting fad. This is the way that humans have eaten for generations.

How a Keto Diet Works

How the Body Handles Carbs

A low-carb diet aims to reduce carbohydrates, which has an important influence on our metabolism. To supply us with energy, our metabolism converts long-chain carbohydrates, such as starch, into glucose molecules. Alternatively, it may store carbohydrates as quickly available power sources in the body—in other words, as glycogen in the liver and muscles. But if these supplies are full, perhaps because they haven't been used up yet, any excess carbohydrates are stored as fat. So if you consume more carbohydrates than you need, the result is that you will gain weight.

This effect is magnified in those diets that consist primarily of sweet items and white flour, and which also lack protein and the fiber that can be found in vegetables. With this kind of diet, carbohydrates and sugar literally rush into the blood, triggering an acute spike in blood sugar levels and forcing the body to respond by vigorously releasing insulin. This insulin causes blood sugar levels to fall rapidly, which in turn triggers an immediate alarm signal: I'm hungry.

The consumption of good-quality fiber, protein, and fat can partially mitigate the effects of sugar and that injection of insulin, but it will not reduce the calories in a carbohydrate-rich diet. Fats and protein even increase the calorie load slightly. So the ideal solution is obvious: avoid those large portions of carbohydrates while also eating more fiber in the form of vegetables and slightly more good fats and protein. That's the idea that lies behind the Keto High Fiber Diet. Furthermore, when carbohydrates are scarce, fat-burning is stimulated. The body begins to produce ketones from fat, which provide energy to the brain and muscles. The stricter the low-carb regimen, the more ketones are produced. This is most pronounced on a keto diet.

How Keto Can Help Diabetes

Since blood sugar levels fluctuate less on a low-carb diet, a low-carb approach is particularly suitable for overweight people with insulin resistance (which is a precursor to Type 2 diabetes) and for diabetics. In our practice, which specializes in the professional treatment of obese patients, we frequently observe that blood sugar levels fall and Type 2 diabetes vanishes after a weight loss of about 5 to 10 percent. A major contributor to this encouraging phenomenon is the way that feelings of intense hunger abate significantly on a low-carb diet, helping our patients to lose weight more easily. This has wonderful results for both their immediate mental and long-term physical well-being.

Why High Fiber Is Important

High fiber means plenty of dietary fiber. Combining high fiber with keto is truly innovative, and this development effectively eliminates the one known drawback for the otherwise healthy low-carb diet. This book is the first to include tasty recipes that are not just low in carbohydrates but are also ketogenic and yet still provide adequate dietary fiber.

Low carb has proven to be a healthy approach to eating, but that isn't the reason this diet is so widespread. Most people who follow this dietary approach want to stay slim or would like to lose weight—and that's where we hit a problem even Atkins recognized: the more we reduce our carbohydrate intake, the more we also miss out on the classic sources of dietary fiber, such as whole-grain products and beans. The result is that the slimming bacteria in the gut are deprived of their superfood.

We should be consuming at least 30g of fiber per day, and for many of us this comes mainly from cereal products. When people transition to a keto diet there is a danger that they will get insufficient fiber, but these consequences are avoidable. With the new Keto High Fiber Diet you can actually significantly improve your gut health. So, what is it about fiber that makes it so special, and what are the benefits?

High Fiber Is Good for the Gut
We consist primarily of bacteria and fungi, at least if you compare the amount of genetic material in these microorganisms with our own. In terms of weight, they make up four and a half pounds of our body weight. They live on all our internal and external surfaces (in other words, on the skin) and, most important, in the gastrointestinal tract, home to 99 percent of these organisms.

Numerically speaking, this equates to one hundred billion microorganisms. Research over the past twenty years has made it increasingly clear how important these intestinal organisms are to us. The reciprocal relationship between human and microbiome plays a central role in preventing and treating illness.

This research has also shown how incorrect it is to suggest that intestinal fungi are inherently harmful, a proposal still being put forward today by certain doctors and alternative medicine practitioners. Intestinal fungi quite clearly play a crucial and beneficial role—they are not always undesirable or harmful. Current research actually shows that fungi in the intestine interact closely with bacteria and perform a vital metabolic role. Consequently, on no account should you try to eradicate these microorganisms.

FIBER'S SPECIAL PROPERTIES

Fiber has so many amazing benefits for your body and the way you feel. Below are just a few of its special properties:

• Fiber can absorb up to one hundred times its own weight in water. In other words, if it is consumed in a dried form (powder), it swells, which is good for the digestive system and for regular bowel movements.

• Because of fiber's propensity to swell, it's essential to consume plenty of liquid at the same time as eating fiber, otherwise stools can become hard and cause constipation. Ultimately, one of the key effects of consuming more fiber in your everyday diet is that it causes stools to spend less time in the bowel.

• Fiber stays in the stomach for a long time because that's where it swells up and increases in volume. This takes some time, which contributes to a feeling of not being hungry for longer. By keeping the stomach full for longer, the hunger hormone (called ghrelin) is inhibited.

• Fiber contains few, if any, calories, largely because the body cannot break it down. Water-insoluble dietary fiber passes through the intestine almost unchanged and undigested. Nevertheless, this fiber aids digestion and creates a sensation of being full.

• Water-soluble fiber, on the other hand, can be fermented by bacteria in the large intestine and thus broken down. This results in the production of odorless gases such as methane, carbon dioxide, and hydrogen.

• The bacteria also create important short-chain fatty acids (SCFAs) such as acetate, propionate, and butyrate. These fatty acids are particularly important because they nourish and support the cells in our intestinal mucous membrane.

The Importance of a Varied Diet

Food components, such as fiber, that are absorbed by the body are prerequisites for the very existence of our microbiome. The more varied our food intake, the greater the range of microorganisms in our gut. We're talking about diversity here: the greater the diversity, the better our health.

There are certain strains of bacteria that tend to keep us slim, while others, such as Firmicutes, will do all they can to extract calories from food. The latter tend to make us fat. A moderate reduction in calories or a diet that is rich in fiber can promote the slimming variety. This effect can lead to weight loss in the longer term.

The Damaging Effects of Antibiotics

Antibiotics have a similarly powerful impact on the microbiome. Until just a few years ago, these drugs were being freely dispensed by my fellow doctors—for example, for flu-like infections. Nowadays, we know better and understand that these illnesses are usually caused by viruses, which cannot be treated with antibiotics anyway.

A harmful feature of antibiotics is that they do not just kill off pathogenic bacteria. In fact, they're pretty indiscriminate in also eradicating lots of useful, beneficial bacteria. When I'm trying to explain this to my patients, I compare the monumental impact of antibiotics to the effect of a bomb going off that cannot distinguish between friend and foe. This disrupts the equilibrium between microorganisms in the gut and on the skin for a considerable period. This, in turn, has many consequences, some of them long-lasting.

The short-term effects of the disruption caused by antibiotics will be familiar to anyone who has been treated with them: digestive problems, diarrhea, constipation, and thrush are possible side effects. All of these are caused by the fact that the microbial equilibrium of the body has been upset.

One of the long-term effects that has been established is that adults who were prescribed lots of antibiotics during childhood and adolescence are significantly more likely to be overweight. Over-prescription appears to favor a selection of bacteria that promotes weight gain.

Macronutrients & Micronutrients

Nutrients can be divided into two categories: macronutrients and micronutrients. Macronutrients make up the majority of our food and are our main source of energy and nutrients. These are carbohydrates, proteins, and fats. Micronutrients are also essential, but are needed in smaller quantities. In terms of carbohydrates—their effect and the tasks they perform in the body—we have pretty much said all there is to say over the previous pages, except for one thing: carbohydrates are the only macronutrients the body can happily do without. That's why a diet without carbohydrates is the number one choice.

By contrast, the body cannot survive without fats, fatty acids, and proteins. These are absolutely essential for our metabolism. The body is also unable to create them itself in the event of a shortfall, which is why many fatty acids and amino acids (the components of proteins) are essential for human life and must be supplied externally.

FATS: GOOD AND BAD

We've gotten used to the terms "good" and "bad" fats, and up until now, it was saturated fats that were regarded as the "bad" fats. However, recent scientific studies have started to change this way of thinking.

What Are Saturated Fats?
The term "saturated" refers to the fats' saturation with hydrogen molecules. This makes them inert and prevents them from forming other chemical compounds, which in turn makes them extremely durable. It is this durability that makes them so popular for use by the food industry—and so easily stored by our bodies.

Since the cell membranes of all our somatic cells consist of fat, if there is too much saturated fat in our diets, the fat metabolism can cause these membranes to become thick and inflexible. After years of consuming saturated fat, our cell walls look like brick walls in which some of the bricks are protruding, some have been pushed back, and some are missing altogether. Among other things, these irregularities predispose us to arteriosclerosis, the thickening of our arteries. Another worrying consequence is poor nutrient exchange, which can result in cells ceasing to function correctly. Saturated fats have another unpleasant characteristic. They can block insulin receptors in individual cells from the inside. The consequence is a permanently elevated blood sugar level or, in other words, diabetes.

THE IMPORTANT TASKS OF FAT IN THE BODY

Fat functions as a fuel

Fatty tissue in humans is actually active tissue, consisting primarily of unsaturated fatty acids like those contained in olive oil and canola oil: fuel that is stored for a brief period. The body needs the energy provided by fat both day and night and lots of the body's repair processes can only take place if fat is available. Fat also tops off the glucose deposits in our muscles. That's why you burn more energy during the regeneration after running than you do during a run. Large muscles require more calories than smaller muscles—and they need this energy twenty-four hours a day, i.e. through the night too.

Fat supports cell growth

The walls of our roughly one hundred trillion cells consist largely of unsaturated fatty acids. These cells undergo constant replacement, around fifty million per second. Fresh supplies of unsaturated fatty acids are required for this to occur. These are mostly runnier than saturated fats, even at low temperatures. That is why fish contain more unsaturated fatty acids than saturated, otherwise they would solidify and stiffen in low water temperatures. For the same reason, eating fish helps us to stay fit and flexible. And it isn't just our cell walls (or cell membranes, to be completely correct) that consist of unsaturated fatty acids, the same is true of our brain cells.

Fat functions as an energy store

Fat can store more energy than either carbohydrates or protein, which explains why the body likes to keep the concentrated energy found in fat in reserve. Saturated fatty acids are also particularly durable, whch is why fats in the stomach are mostly stored as saturated fat.

Saturated fats are also powerful signaling substances—with a damaging impact if available in excess quantities. Research has shown that clinically obese patients have up to five times the quantity of inflammatory substances in their blood (including interleukin 6 and other immune cells) as other people. Abdominal fat specifically functions as a kind of hormonal gland, sending out harmful messengers. Overweight people who don't get enough exercise are particularly badly affected. Cancers of the prostate, colon, breast, and ovaries all increase proportionately with the consumption of fatty acids, as do heart disease, stroke, and even Alzheimer's. In overweight people with comorbidities, up to 40 percent of cells in their fatty tissues are not fat cells but inflammatory cells. The proportion of saturated fat in our bodies is directly linked to our diet. If the body is supplied with excessive amounts, the proportion of saturated fat in the body rises and, accordingly, so does the number of localized inflammation points. However, this does not mean that we can, or indeed should, completely eliminate saturated fat.

According to the very latest research, saturated fats are not intrinsically bad. On the contrary, the important factor is their ratio to unsaturated fats in the diet and not consuming them to excess.

Trans Fats Are Bad Fats

Trans fats are produced when unsaturated fatty acids are made more durable (through hydrogenation), and they are unequivocally harmful. Trans fats are found in lots of mass-produced foods (fried products, ready meals, potato chips, cookies, pastry, and ice cream). At one point, margarine also contained a large number of trans fats, but nowadays these have been reduced to a minimum. Make sure you avoid heating your oil for frying beyond its smoke point. If the oil is smoking in the pan, it is already carcinogenic.

Good Fats

Plants predominantly contain unsaturated fatty acids. These are easily absorbed by the body, offer an efficient source of fuel, and are excellent building materials for strong cells and tissues. These so-called good fats also provide the fat-soluble vitamins A, D, E, and K to support a healthy metabolism, and thus a good supply of somatic cells. Good fats include so-called unsaturated and polyunsaturated fatty acids. Unsaturated fatty acids (for example, olive oil) are easy to recognize by the fact that they are liquid at room temperature. Polyunsaturated fats (for example, wheatgerm oil and flaxseed oil) are always liquid in form.

Good Fats Are Particularly Found In:

- nuts
- seeds
- olive oil
- almond oil
- peanut oil
- wheatgerm oil
- canola oil
- flaxseed oil
- avocados
- meat from free-range game
- fatty fish, such as salmon
  and mackerel

Early humans got 30 percent of their energy from fats, although back then—in contrast to today—these would have been exclusively good fats. So, why is there more saturated fat in food these days? Free-range venison has just 10 percent fat, predominantly unsaturated, but when animals are kept on an industrial scale, they aren't able to move as much; they're fattened up, and the proportion of fat goes up to 30 percent. The quality of the fat also declines. It is largely saturated.

What Are the Benefits of Good Fats?

One particularly important characteristic of good fats is that when you eat them with carbohydrates, the fats prevent these carbohydrates from being broken down too quickly into sugar molecules, thus protecting us against elevated blood sugar levels and the subsequent powerful insulin response. That's why white bread, such as ciabatta or baguettes (which are far from recommended with the keto approach), should always be eaten with a bit of olive oil—just as they are in Mediterranean cuisine. Of course, you can always choose a different kind of oil or perhaps eat an avocado alongside.

Omega-3 Fatty Acids

Omega-3 fatty acids are predominantly found in oily fish and have long been regarded as especially healthy. They inhibit the development of inflammatory substances in the body and offer natural protection against the inflammatory response that underlies many conditions, not least arteriosclerosis. Omega-3 fatty acids, in particular, keep cell membranes supple and guarantee a normal supply of somatic cells. People living in areas where a lot of fish is eaten are less susceptible to lifestyle illnesses such as cardiovascular disease, rheumatism, and allergies than are those who do not eat fish. Recent studies have shown that fish is a better option than blends of omega-3 fatty acids in capsule form. This seems to be very similar to the added value offered by fruit in comparison to vitamin supplements.

PROTEIN: THE BUILDING BLOCKS

Proteins are essential for life. From hormones, skin, and hair to muscles, over half of your body's weight (if you disregard water) consists of protein. Apart from water, which makes up 60 to 70 percent of your weight, proteins are the most commonly found substance in the body. Among other things, they are vital for the development of tissues and organs, our immune response system, blood clotting, control of gene activity, and many other functions. High-quality protein is also crucial for keeping insulin and blood glucose in equilibrium. When protein is metabolized, the hormone glucagon is released, which counteracts the effects of insulin. If consumed alongside carbohydrates, protein ensures insulin and blood sugar levels remain stable, which is crucial for our health and weight. There are good reasons for supplying the body with high-quality protein—especially as the body cannot produce at least eight of the total of twenty amino acids from which it assembles its own proteins. These amino acids have to be consumed as part of our daily diet in order to avoid the risk of any deficiency. Insufficient protein has a negative impact on weight because if the body gets too little protein, it starts breaking down muscle to obtain it, replacing that muscle with fat. A shortage of protein is linked with additional body fat.

Sources of Protein—There Are Good and Bad
A fundamental principle is that protein from animals is biologically higher in quality than plant-based protein. When we talk about quality, this means more physical structures can be created in the body from the same amount of protein. Try to choose organic products when buying meat. This may be more expensive, but there are several benefits, as organic produce contains significantly healthier fats and no antibiotics.

Good Sources of Protein:
- poultry (chicken and turkey, including the fatty skin)
- fish (salmon, mackerel, tuna, and other oily varieties of fish)
- lean meat (especially beef and lamb)
- lean ham
- cheese and eggs
- soy and tofu

Unprocessed Meat Is Better

Fatty hams and sausages should be avoided because their protein content is lower than in unadulterated meat. This is due to the abundance of fillers: carbohydrates, fat, spices, flavor enhancers, and salts in the form of nitrates and nitrites. Extensive processing means that sausage products are also associated with an increased risk of cancer. One very good source of protein is oily fish, because it contains some particularly valuable omega-3 fatty acids.

MICRONUTRIENTS

In recent years, scientists have been looking closely at an additional group of nutrients alongside crucial vitamins and minerals. These are the so-called secondary plant substances. We now recognize several thousand substances that all play a vital role in the body's ongoing repair and defense systems. These are micronutrients.

Micronutrients strengthen the immune system against harmful viruses, fungi, and bacteria; protect the circulation system and blood vessels; and combat the common problem of oxidative stress. This oxidative stress is triggered by so-called free radicals.

These aggressive compounds of otherwise essential oxygen can cause all sorts of harm to the body—including damage to our genetic material, which in turn can impair cell performance or even trigger the harmful creation of cancer cells. One example is tomatoes, which contain lycopene. This can trap radicals and neutralize aggressive oxygen. Laboratory tests have successfully shown that lycopene is able to prevent certain cancer cells from connecting to the blood supply and thus can inhibit their growth. To improve your vision, you should be eating plenty of kale, spinach, and broccoli, as these vegetables contain the micronutrients zeaxanthin and lutein. There has also been a particular interest in the suggested protective antioxidant and anti-inflammatory effect offered by a specific flavonoid—resveratrol—primarily found in red grapes. Some is also contained in red wine.

While many vitamins can be made synthetically, nutritional supplements are devoid of the great wealth of micronutrients. Vegetables, fruit, herbs, salads, nuts, seeds, shoots, meat, and fish, with all their precious substances, cannot simply be replicated in tablet form. That is why natural, unprocessed foods are extremely important on the Keto High Fiber Diet and should make up the lion's share of your diet.

The Benefits of the Keto High Fiber Diet

Less Hunger
Diets that leave you hungry will not work. Ever. Hunger is such a powerful, fe-threatening signal that nobody can overcome it for long. The Keto High Fiber Diet approach is particularly effective against hunger. Fiber makes you feel fuller, so hunger cravings between meals don't stand a chance. Carbohydrates are also replaced with protein and fat on this diet and, because the body takes longer to digest these, you feel full for longer. By consuming fewer short-chain carbohydrates (e.g., white flour, sugar) you stabilize your blood sugar levels, which prevents your feeling hungry and improves the chances of success with changing eating habits. Keto diets keep you feeling full for longer. Keto High Fiber enhances this effect even further.

"The Keto High Fiber Diet Effect"
Gradual alterations in the microbiome through the increased consumption of dietary fiber result in a rise in the number of slimming bacteria. This means fewer calories are absorbed from the meals consumed.

Deep Abdominal Fat Melts Away
Visceral fat is deposited around the internal organs and is particularly dangerous. It produces hormones, chemical messengers that can make us ill in the long term. Consequences include high blood pressure, elevated blood lipid values, and diabetes. It has been shown that low-carb diets break down fat significantly better than other diets, bringing demonstrable health benefits.

Cholesterol Levels Improve
HDL is a lipoprotein and transport vehicle that ensures cholesterol in the body is taken to the liver. It's a cleansing agent, unclogging arteries (think "H" for "healthy" to remember that HDL is the good cholesterol). The lipoprotein LDL triggers the opposite process, resulting in arteriosclerosis, or vascular calcification. In addition to LDL, there are other lipoproteins that are detrimental to health, and we refer to these collectively as non-HDL. The ratio of HDL to non-HDL is crucial and can be improved by a low-carb diet with plenty of healthy fats. Thanks to the increased excretion of bile acids, fiber also lowers cholesterol.

Dangerous Triglycerides in the Bloodstream Are Reduced
When it comes to fat, everyone knows the significance of cholesterol. There is good (HDL) and bad (LDL or non-HDL). But there is another kind of fat—triglyceride—which is just as important. Triglycerides are fat molecules that significantly increase the risk of a heart attack. People today have too much sugar and fat in their blood,

particularly triglycerides. When someone says they have "high blood fat levels," many people think "Well, just eat less fat." But this rarely works for weight loss or for reducing triglycerides. Limiting carbohydrates is a far more effective way, as is reducing alcohol, I should point out! Both of these are converted into triglycerides in the body, then transferred into the blood, where they are directed to tissues and cells.

Keto Diets Lower Blood Sugar Levels
All carbohydrates have one thing in common, even those in whole grains: they are broken down into short-chain glucose molecules, and, depending on the quantity, this causes a rise in blood sugar and thus also a rise in insulin levels. High blood sugar levels cause our arteries to become clogged more quickly, in the same way hard water causes deposits to build up in pipes. Insulin is a growth hormone that not only promotes the growth of healthy cells but also, unfortunately, bad cells, including those that fuel arteriosclerosis and allow the development of cancer cells. A low-carb diet reduces this effect. In diabetics, this can mean they need less insulin, or maybe none at all. Once again, fiber helps even out spikes in blood sugar levels and thus also reduces the insulin response.

Improvements in Metabolic Syndrome (a Lifestyle Illness)
Metabolic syndrome is characterized by increased abdominal girth, high blood pressure, elevated cholesterol and triglyceride values, and insulin resistance. Each of these conditions on its own is bad for our health, but in combination the effect is worse, with the result that arteriosclerosis increases dramatically, making heart attacks and strokes more likely. Rates of cancer also go up. A diet that is low in carbs, combined with plenty of fiber, has a positive impact on metabolic syndrome.

Good for the Brain
It appears that part of the human brain depends exclusively on glucose to function properly, while other areas can clearly use ketones. Even if there are some parts of the brain that still need glucose, this does not have to be supplied by carbohydrates. In fact, the liver is able to obtain glucose from protein to ensure these parts of the brain receive the necessary supply. Scientists are currently researching how a keto diet can impact illnesses that are associated with carbohydrates. It has already proven to be beneficial for children suffering from epilepsy and for the treatment of Alzheimer's, multiple sclerosis, and Parkinson's.

Why Ketosis?

In a ketogenic diet, carbohydrate intake should be between 25g (strict) and 50g (moderate). If you reduce your intake even further, this prevents the consumption of fundamentally healthy foods such as berries, which would be counterproductive from a health perspective.

Ketosis is an alternative option for the body to create energy. In ketosis you primarily burn fat instead of sugar. It's important to clarify here that this has nothing to do with ketoacidosis, a serious condition that can affect diabetics, in which ketones and sugar end up in the bloodstream because the body cannot process sugar due to a lack of insulin, for instance, or because the insulin is ineffective.

In ketosis, fat is transformed into ketones, which the body can convert into energy in the same way as it can with sugar. This occurs during periods of starvation and also if there is insufficient or minimal carbohydrate consumption. The body needs a couple of days to perform this conversion because it first needs to produce the necessary enzymes. Ketones actually supply more energy than glucose. For instance, the brain needs just 40g of ketones to match 120g of glucose.

As long as sugar or stored sugar (glycogen) is available, the body will burn this in preference to ketones from its fat deposits or from fat consumed. Only once this sugar has been burned and no more is eaten does the body initiate its own weight-loss program: ketosis. In other words, fat does not make us fat.

When insulin levels are low, the fat cells open up and release their stores of fatty acids. The liver converts these into ketone bodies. Ketones constitute ideal, constant fuel for the heart and brain and for nearly all other cells in the body. Their consistency is due to the fact that the energy production from ketones does not depend on insulin. There are no peaks and valleys like there are when burning sugar. This is also the reason why a ketogenic diet is beneficial for so many health conditions: insulin insensitivity has been established as a precondition for Type 2 diabetes, multiple sclerosis, and Parkinson's. This means insulin can no longer channel sugar into the cells. The consequence is an inadequate energy supply to the cells, which exacerbates the illness. Ketones restore the energy supply to these cells.

Top athletes are also taking advantage of this phenomenon, many of them with the same performance formula: no carbs! Increasing numbers of high-profile celebrities are also converting to a low-carbohydrate diet with amazing results. Renouncing carbohydrates permanently is really hard, but a twenty-eight-day carbohydrate fast each year is certainly achievable.

BENEFITS OF A KETO DIET FOR SPORTS

There are some real benefits to following the Keto High Fiber Diet if you enjoy general physical exercise and sports, whether you're a professional athlete or just like to kick a ball around in your yard.

Moderate physical activity is an extremely important part of promoting good health, both physically and mentally, and these many benefits extend into everyday life too. The benefits include:

• Increased fat burning and thus improved stamina during training.

• Enhanced mental capacity and clarity—whether in sports or for your job.

• Weight loss and thus an improved body composition, which among many other benefits will also enhance performance ability for all sports.

• For endurance sports, such as running, there should be no so-called hitting the wall after nine or ten miles. In other words, there will be no sudden slump in performance caused by a carbohydrate depletion.

• There is no need to take packs of carbohydrates or glucose tablets to consume during sports to keep your body's deposits topped up.

• A low-carbohydrate diet provides the body with a quicker recovery time after both intense and more relaxed training sessions or other physical activity.

• The ketogenic diet is anti-inflammatory.

The Two Phases of the Keto High Fiber Diet

The twenty-eight-day keto phase of this diet is split in two, with an intense keto boost to start, then a moderate stabilization phase.

Phase 1: Keto Boost

Let's start with the initial ketogenic phase, the keto boost. For the first few days, just 20g of carbohydrates per day is allowed. That is very little. In the next phase, the general rule is 25 or sometimes 30g. I recommend 20g initially, then 30g from the fourth day. To compensate, you can consume larger quantities of protein in the form of fish, meat, eggs, and tofu. You can also eat plenty of salads and certain vegetables. And, of course, you can eat fats and oils. If your previous diet consisted primarily of short-chain carbohydrates—i.e., sugar—you may experience withdrawal symptoms for two to three days. During this phase your sugar stores (or glycogen deposits) are emptying and no longer being topped up. At first this can make you feel as though you lack energy, but that soon changes. And in exchange, you swiftly lose four and a half pounds of water, which was bound up with glycogen. Write down your aims for changing your diet. Do you want to feel fitter and healthier? Have more energy? Or is your main objective losing weight? It's best to express these goals in the present tense. This helps underscore that your goals are achievable and not a pipe dream for an unspecified point in the future.

Day 1
Find recipes that are very low in carbohydrates for breakfast and lunch. On the first day, skip the evening meal, if possible, or eat a salad with a very small steak or fish.

Day 2
Start with one or two glasses of water. This stimulates your circulation and promotes digestion. If you enjoy exercise, it would be great to do a training session on an empty stomach to deplete your glycogen stores further. If nothing else, you should go for a walk. Don't be surprised if you feel less energetic than usual. Stick to your very low-carb recipes and focus on the balance between carbohydrates (ideally just 20 to 25g) and dietary fiber (depending on what you're used to, up to 25g).

Day 3
Start with water. Physical activity before breakfast is a great plan. Glycogen stores are almost depleted. Your performance level may fall, but ketosis is firing up.

Days 4 to 14
Generally from the fourth day your energy returns, and often you'll feel stronger than before. To remain in ketosis, do not exceed 25 to 30g of carbohydrates. And don't go overboard with protein (avoid big portions of meat, fish, tofu, etc.), as the body can produce carbohydrates from it. Because this diet makes you feel full for longer, many people find they get by with two meals per day. This constitutes an ideal meal frequency, but three is also okay. Do not exceed 30g of carbohydrates.

Phase 2: Stabilization

Now you can continue with a moderate ketogenic approach. During this phase, your carbohydrate intake can be slightly increased from 25 to 30g to a maximum of 50g of carbohydrates per day, provided you continue to stay in ketosis. If you ever feel you may have slipped out of ketosis, you can check this by using testing strips (see below) and, if necessary, resume the strict Phase 1 regimen for a minimum of three days. The problem with a keto diet is that just one meal that is high in carbohydrates can catapult you straight out of ketosis. Whereas other diets can accommodate the occasional relapse, unfortunately with ketosis you have to be very disciplined to avoid having to start all over again. Because the twenty-eight-day period has a clearly defined end point, it's easier to stick to the principles and experience the many benefits of the keto diet.

Basic Principles for Both Phases
These are for a bit more flexibility, especially if you don't always follow the recipes:
- Only eat foods that have less than 5g of carbohyrates per 100g.
- Don't overdo protein: 2g per 2.2 pounds of body weight is the limit. So a 176-pound man can consume up to 160g of protein, especially if he is physically active. The tastiest option is to meet these requirements from dairy, fish, and tofu.
- Eat enough fat to feel full. This won't be easy after years of low-fat brainwashing, but don't worry—it won't make you put on weight. You can use fats and oils with a healthy combination of saturated and unsaturated fatty acids, such as canola, olive, and flaxseed oils and, yes, butter.

When Am I in Ketosis?
The most reliable way to measure ketones is in your blood, and devices to do this can be bought in pharmacies. But other indications can be used too:
- Less hunger and fewer sweet cravings, as well as more energy ketones on your breath (a sweet mouth odor).
- A rapid weight loss of four and a half pounds, because carbohydrates are bound up with water.
- Test strips to measure ketones in your urine (though not as precise as blood).

In the Long Term
After you have finished Phase 2, the best approach is to be flexible with the amount of carbohydrates you consume. It isn't necessary to drastically reduce carbohydrates on a permanent basis. To minimize relapses with a low-carb approach, I recommend adjusting carbohydrate levels depending on your weight and physical activity. So once you have achieved your target weight and incorporated regular physical activity into your lifestyle, you can eat more carbohydrates.

DR. KURSCHEID COOKS

For me, it's crucial to have a light and healthy midday meal that is quick and easy to prepare. Light means it shouldn't trigger an afternoon slump, but will keep me fit and healthy. That's why I cook for myself at my practice at lunchtime.

You might find that surprising, but it really is possible. This is how I do it: I always have frozen vegetables and fish in the freezer at my clinic. I put both into pans on my hotplate, then pop on the lids. While these thaw over medium heat, I go back to my desk to continue working. Total time required: no more than two minutes. After ten minutes I take a peek. If everything has defrosted, I turn the fish over, stir the vegetables, and increase the temperature slightly. I then add pepper, salt, and maybe some chives, drizzle lemon over the fish, and turn off the heat. Actual time required: less than five minutes. I generally eat in the kitchen while chatting with my colleagues, or sometimes I enjoy my meal alone. Either way I don't go on my smartphone or read at the same time. After all, this is my daily oasis of relaxation and enjoyment—and I need it.

DR. KURSCHEID'S SUPER-FIBER RAW FOOD

Chop 4½ ounces peeled carrots in a food processor to the size of bulgar wheat or rice grains, then drizzle with 4 teaspoons lime juice. Sprinkle in 2 tablespoons flaxseed meal, 1 tablespoon chia seeds, 2 tablespoons almond meal, 1½ tablespoons dry unsweetened coconut, and ¼ ounce inulin and combine. Finally, stir in 2 teaspoons wheatgerm oil.

This provides 410 calories, 13g protein, 33g fat, 9g carbohydrate, and 25.5g fiber.

TIP
Due to the particularly high quantity of fiber, this raw food recipe is a great option if you are struggling to get the usual amount of fiber for the day, including when you're traveling. Since the chia seeds aren't soaked beforehand, it's important to consume plenty of liquid with this dish.

The Best High-Fiber Foods for a Keto Diet

To maintain a healthy gut and good digestion, a minimum of 25 to 30g of fiber per day is recommended. To achieve this, usually whole wheat bread, beans, and dried fruit are specified—however, these are anything but low carb. So for Keto High Fiber the goal was to

RECOMMENDED INGREDIENTS

You won't be able to buy all these ingredients at your local grocery store. When sourcing ingredients, we recommend large grocery stores, health-food stores, or looking online. Carbohydrates and fiber are given in parentheses. Figures are rounded to the nearest value and refer to 100g of each product.

Almond meal	(7g carbs, 19g fiber)
Chia flour	(3g carbs, 46g fiber)
Coconut flour	(4g carbs, 34g fiber)
Insulin	(8g carbs, 92g fiber)
Flaxseed flour	(0g carbs, 48g fiber)
Potato fibers	(8g carbs, 65g fiber)
Psyllium fiber powder	(2g carbs, 85g fiber)

FRUIT & VEGETABLES

Blueberries	(6g carbs, 5 g fiber)
Broccoli, cauliflower	(2.5g carbs, 3g fiber)
Celery root	(2.5g carbs, 4g fiber)
Jerusalem artichokes	(4g carbs, 12g fiber)
Kale	(2.5g carbs, 4.5g fiber)
Oyster mushrooms	(0g carbs, 6g fiber)
Peppers	(3g carbs, 6g fiber)
Raspberries	(5g carbs, 5g fiber)
Spinach	(0.5g carbs, 2.5g fiber)

These vegetables are low carb, but have very little fiber:

Arugula	(2g carbs, 1.5g fiber)
Lettuce	(2g carbs, 1.5g fiber)
Tomatoes	(2.5g carbs, 1g fiber)
Zucchini	(2g carbs, 1g fiber)

AVOCADO

This is the perfect Keto High-Fiber fruit. With a fat content of almost 24g, plus 0.5g of carbohydrate and 6g of fiber, the avocado is unbeatable and also very versatile. Add it to a morning bowl, a salad, or a veggie stir-fry, or use as a spread.

NUTS

Almonds	(4g carbs, 14g fiber)
Cashews	(30g carbs, 3g fiber)
Hazelnuts	(10.5g carbs, 8g fiber)
Macadamia nuts	(4g carbs, 11.5g fiber)
Pecans	(4.5g carbs, 9.5g fiber)
Unsweetened coconut	(8g carbs, 24g fiber)
Walnuts	(10.5g carbs, 6g fiber)

SEEDS

Chia	(4.5g carbs, 37g fiber)
Hemp seeds, hulled	(2g carbs, 4g fiber)
Hemp seeds, unhulled	(3g carbs, 31g fiber)
Flaxseed, brown	(0g carbs, 35g fiber)
Flaxseed, golden	(0g carbs, 35g fiber)
Poppy seeds	(4g carbs, 20.5g fiber)

OILS

For frying, coconut or peanut oil are ideal, as they tolerate high temperatures. For cold dishes, use cold-pressed olive oil, canola, wheatgerm, or flaxseed oil (stored in the dark).

find foods that are rich in fiber while also being low in carbohydrates. These ingredients can then be combined in delicious quick-and-easy recipes. This approach combines the healthy low-carb diet with a gut-friendly one—something that wasn't available before.

EGGS

Eggs are ideal despite having a keto factor of just 65. By frying eggs in some oil or butter, you can bring them into the ketogenic range.

INULIN

Inulin is an insider tip when it comes to dietary fiber. A soft, slightly sweet powder obtained from Jerusalem artichokes or chicory, it is wonderful stirred into yogurt, soup, or a sauce. Usually a teaspoon (5 to 6g) is a sufficient quantity, as this alone contains 5g of fiber. For some recipes, inulin is an integral component, as the other ingredients do not contain enough fiber. In other recipes it's optional. So during the first phase, you can omit the inulin, then subsequently include it to achieve the desired quantity of fiber.

PSYLLIUM FIBER POWDER

This has a powerful capacity to retain water, which is why it's not as pleasant in yogurt as inulin. This same characteristic makes it the perfect ingredient for baking bread.

INCREASING FIBER INTAKE

When converting to the Keto High Fiber Diet, you should take your time to adjust to the recommended daily quantities of 25 to 30g of fiber: not everyone can tolerate these amounts immediately. Once your gut has gotten used to this, the quantity of fiber will be increased to 35 to 40g over the next fourteen days.

THE KETO FACTOR

A recipe is ketogenic if at least 70 percent of the calories come from fats. Next to each recipe, I have indicated the keto factor, which I initially calculated simply to check that at least 70 percent of the calories really do come from fat. For example, if the factor is 72, it means that 72 percent of the calories are from fat. This value becomes especially important if you want to add or substitute another ingredient. If the keto factor is low, it should be a high-fat food like a piece of avocado, not carbohydrates or fiber, as that would drop the factor below 70 and the recipe would no longer be ketogenic.

OUR KETO HIGH-FIBER BREADS

The bread recipes in the book are intrinsically ketogenic; 70 percent or more of their calories come from fat. So these breads go beautifully without any toppings, with a salad or soup, without the keto factor going below 70.

HAVEN'T ALWAYS GOT TIME TO COOK?

Most recipes are ready in fifteen minutes, some take twenty, and some can be prepared even faster. But if you haven't managed to shop, a supply of Keto High-Fiber breads is really helpful. After baking, just slice the cooled bread and freeze it between sheets of parchment paper in an airtight container. Then you can remove slices and quickly defrost them in the toaster. And for a topping, try to have an avocado on hand: just mash it straight onto the bread with a fork. Salt, pepper, maybe a tomato, too, and it's ready.

Keeping on Track

Once you've stayed the course for twenty-eight days, everything will feel much easier. In order to stay slim and healthy, incorporate as many of the guidelines that follow into your everyday life as you can:

Mindfulness When Eating

Mindfulness means switching off from autopilot mode. Focus on just one thing and give it your exclusive, deliberate attention, especially when you're eating. By doing this, you will find out that feeling full has less to do with the size of the portion and more to do with the impact of the experience. Mindfulness when eating means being present when you're consuming food and really listening to your body to be clear about the following question: Why am I eating now?

Emotional hunger feels different from genuine hunger. When you're genuinely hungry, your stomach grumbles below the solar plexus. The sensation for emotional hunger is located higher and is often described as "above the neck." From now on, before every meal or snack, say to yourself: "Stop." First listen to your body. Don't let your body translate all its emotions into the single language of (supposed) hunger, which you then immediately respond to with food. Regard hunger as a sign of your internal feelings. Recognize that eating in response to an emotional deficit will not really help and is more likely to add to your problems. If appropriate, seek professional help.

Eat More Slowly to Become Full More Quickly

People who eat quickly fill up their stomachs quickly, but they don't feel full any faster. It takes twenty minutes for the stomach to signal to the brain that it is replete. Until then, you keep eating, and you may end up consuming far more than you wanted to. Too late for regrets. You feel absolutely stuffed and slightly unwell, and you will have stretched your stomach, too. By contrast, the more slowly you eat and the better you chew your food, the quicker you will feel full and satisfied. Try the following experiment: chew for a really long time on some whole wheat bread. What happens to the flavor? Correct: it becomes sweeter. This is because the digestive enzymes in your mouth break down starch in the bread into sugar. This is channeled straight into your bloodstream via the mucosa and immediately signals to the brain: "You can rein in the hunger pangs, I'm already half full." Moreover, by eating slowly you prolong enjoyment, and blood sugar levels won't rise steeply.

No Snacking

The longer you can keep your insulin levels low, the better it is for fat burning. Consequently, it seems to be beneficial to restrict your window for eating to eight hours per day and to go sixteen hours without eating. One schedule might look like this: breakfast around 10 a.m. and an evening meal at 6 p.m. You'll find this easy to stick to on a low-carb regime, and particularly with a keto approach, because the high levels of fiber, fat, and protein consumed keep you feeling full for longer than will a diet that is rich in carbohydrates.

You'll also notice that snack cravings between meals diminish significantly. Be strict about avoiding snacks during phases 1 and 2. All calories count here, even if they sound healthy or seem really small and insignificant. In the evening, our metabolism slows down. As a result, evening consumption of foods that are rich in carbohydrates, particularly sugary items, causes a 7 percent higher rise in blood sugar levels, and this spike lasts longer, too.

Avoid Hunger Pangs by Eating More Wisely

Once hunger strikes, it's very hard to resist, because the brain goes into emergency mode, screaming "I need sugar!" Even after a large meal, you're left feeling like you really could finish with something else (preferably sweet). That's why eating at fixed times is important, as is focusing on foods that will keep you feeling full. In other words, Keto High Fiber. But once hunger has struck, what should you do?

The first thing to try is drinking a glass of water. Then eat a soup or salad before you start on the main course. People who drink regularly will find it easier to lose weight than those who fail to drink enough. There are two reasons for this. First, people who drink plenty of water don't get hungry as easily. Secondly, the body burns an additional 100 calories per 35 ounces of water consumed. This is because it uses calories warming the water, metabolizing it, and excreting it. So, in the future, if you drink 100 ounces of water rather than 70 ounces, you will burn a total of 36,000 extra calories over the course of a year—that's equivalent to eleven fewer pounds of fatty tissue in your body.

Plenty of Physical Activity

Someone who is overweight but exercises regularly will have a healthier life than a thin person who fails to exercise. Remember: physical activity doesn't just use more energy and keep you slim; there are other benefits. Exercise lowers blood pressure (strength training has the same effect); keeps your blood vessels flexible and youthful; prevents diabetes and metabolic syndrome, and hence also cardiovascular disease and cancer; improves mental capabilities; strengthens tendons, joints, and bones; and lowers the risk of osteoporosis. And best of all, it's fun and free. The ideal is a combination of endurance and strength training.

As Little Alcohol as Possible

Avoid alcohol completely during phases 1 and 2, as it is no secret that it's high in calories. Nonetheless, people often underestimate the true number. White wine contains more calories than cola drinks or fruit juice. Thirty-five ounces of dry white wine with 12 percent alcohol comes to 800 calories; a medium-dry red wine with 12.5 percent alcohol comes to almost 1,000 calories. Calories from alcohol end up predominantly as abdominal fat, which is particularly harmful due to its hormone production. Since alcohol is also a toxin, the body focuses on breaking this down before it tackles the remaining calories and fuel—and you get plenty of the latter because many people experience powerful food cravings caused by fluctuating insulin levels. You also sleep less well; although you might fall asleep faster, your sleep becomes fragmented because you no longer go into deep sleep.

Good Sleep is Vital

Avoid stimulants like TV and caffeinated beverages immediately before going to bed. In the evening, write out a plan for the next day to clear your head. You also sleep less well on a full stomach. Ideally you should avoid eating for three or four hours before going to sleep. Always try to go to bed at the same time, and substitute watching TV with a relaxing habit like walking, listening to soothing music, taking a bath, or drinking herbal tea (no black or green teas, as these are stimulants). You should try to create a darker environment around you even before you go to bed, and the bedroom should be dark to help the body produce melatonin, the sleep hormone. Your sleeping environment should be quiet; even sounds that don't wake us up can trigger a stress response, which raises your blood pressure.

Regular Check-ups

This book's twenty-eight-day keto program should enable you to tackle any weight gain immediately. But don't just rely on your body's early warning systems; your body cannot always notify you about increases in blood sugar, cholesterol, and blood pressure. That's why you need to be alert to any fat deposits around your midriff. This is an indication that something is happening internally as well as externally. Check your blood sugar levels regularly, and make sure your biannual checkups include a review of cholesterol, triglyceride, and blood pressure levels.

HOW TO MAKE A SUCCESSSFUL START

• Write down your goals and look at them regularly.

• Prepare well. Get the most important groceries that you can't get in the grocery store beforehand on the internet or in a health-food store. Buy a precise digital scale for food and a good bathroom scale, preferably a bioimpedance scale.

• Weigh yourself several times in advance at different times of the day and note your weight. Use a tape measure to take your waist circumference. Take pictures of yourself.

• Sort out foods that have lots of carbohydrates. Put them away or give them away.

• Start by eating no more than 20g of carbohydrates and about 10 to 20g of fiber for the first few days until you feel that you are in ketosis. If you stick to these recipes—even with three meals in combination—you cannot consume too many carbohydrates.

• Now increase the carbohydrates to a maximum of 50g per day. At the same time, try to increase the fiber to 35 to 40g. Do not allow exceptions. If you've consumed too many carbohydrates, you will need to start from scratch.

• Do not be discouraged if you're a little tired or have mild complaints in the first four days.

• If you get the feeling that you are about to become weak, distract yourself for ten to twenty minutes and drink a glass of water. That is almost always enough to get rid of such thoughts. These thoughts are completely normal—even the most disciplined person has them—but distraction helps.

• For any invitations out, it's best to bring something that suits your diet—for example, a salad. The same applies when you're on the go or in the office. With a reserve of hard-boiled eggs, a few olives, or suitable nuts, you can get over any lows.

(V) beside a recipe identifies a vegetarian dish
(VE) beside a recipe identifies a vegan dish
(GF) beside a recipe identifies a gluten-free dish

Recipes

Here are 69 recipes, with lots of vegetarian, vegan, and gluten-free choices that can be mixed and matched for breakfast, lunch, and dinner.

Phase 1:
Keto Boost

Here we go. With good preparation, you'll be able to switch from glucose fuel to ketone super-fuel.

Maximum of 25 to 30g of carbohydrates
and 25 to 30g of fiber per day

Morning Bowl with Strawberries, Avocado & Cottage Cheese

Per portion: 387 calories, 17g protein, 32g fat, 8g carbohydrate, 10g fiber | Keto factor: 74

SERVES 1
Prep: 5 minutes

½ large avocado
1 teaspoon lime juice
½ cup cottage cheese
¼ cup unsweetened
   shredded coconut
¾ cup strawberries, chopped

1 Remove the flesh from the avocado using a spoon, dice, place in a serving bowl, and drizzle with the lime juice.

2 Mix the cottage cheese with the shredded coconut. Arrange in the bowl with the avocado and strawberries.

Want more fiber?
Mix an additional 1½ teaspoons inulin with the cottage cheese. This results in 392 calories, 17g protein, 32g fat, 8g carbohydrate, and 14g fiber per portion (Keto factor: 73).

Morning Bowl with Chia & Coconut

Per portion: 438 calories, 20g protein, 36g fat, 7g carbohydrate, 8g fiber | Keto factor: 74

SERVES 1
Prep: 5 minutes
Chia: 30 minutes (or overnight)

1 tablespoon chia seeds
½ cup quark (20% fat) or full-fat
   cream cheese
¼ cup full-fat coconut milk
1 teaspoon wheatgerm oil
1 teaspoon lime juice
pinch of ground cinnamon or
   1 teaspoon vanilla extract
¼ cup unsweetened
   shredded coconut
1 teaspoon grated lime zest
pinch of salt

1 Add the chia seeds to a bowl, stir in 1 to 2 teaspoons warm water, and soak for at least 30 minutes, or overnight.

2 The next morning, mix the quark or cream cheese with the coconut milk, wheatgerm oil, and lime juice and stir into the chia seeds. Season with the cinnamon or vanilla.

3 Mix the shredded coconut with the lime zest and salt and sprinkle over the bowl.

Tip
It's best to buy coconut milk with a 70 to 90 percent coconut extract without binders and additives. Any leftover coconut milk can be frozen. Stir well and separate into ¼-cup or ½-cup portions, pop into small freezer containers, and freeze.

Morning Bowl with Egg, Tomato & Avocado

Per portion: 471 calories, 16g protein, 42g fat, 6g carbohydrate, 9g fiber | Keto factor: 80

SERVES 1

Prep: 15 minutes

FOR THE BOWL

1 large egg

1 small avocado

½ teaspoon lime juice

⅔ cup cherry tomatoes, halved

salt and freshly ground black pepper

1 small bunch fresh flat-leaf parsley,
  leaves chopped

FOR THE PASTE

3 teaspoons tomato paste

1 teaspoon olive oil

½ to 1 teaspoon sambal oelek

pinch of ground cumin

salt and freshly ground black pepper

Spice up the morning with a good grind of pepper—very alkaline—a good squeeze of lime, and a magic paste using sambal oelek and cumin.

1 For the bowl, cook the egg in a pan of boiling water for 6 minutes for soft-boiled or 10 minutes for hard-boiled, whichever you prefer. Peel and cut into quarters.

2 For the paste, mix the tomato paste with the oil and sambal oelek, then add the cumin and season with salt and freshly ground black pepper. Work in 1 to 2 teaspoons of water.

3 Remove the flesh from the avocado using a spoon, cut into wedges, drizzle with the lime juice, and arrange in a serving bowl next to the tomatoes and egg.

4 Season everything lightly, then dollop the tomato paste over the top and sprinkle with the chopped parsley.

Morning Bowl with Cucumber, Radish & Pistachio Pesto

Per portion: 354 calories, 6g protein, 34g fat, 7.5g carbohydrate, 9g fiber | Keto factor: 86

SERVES 1
Prep: 10 to 15 minutes

FOR THE BOWL
1 to 2 mini cucumbers, sliced
1 medium (1½lb) daikon radish,
    peeled and sliced
½ avocado, sliced
salt and freshly ground black pepper
1 teaspoon lime juice

FOR THE PESTO
1 small bunch fresh parsley, leaves
    finely chopped
¼ cup pistachios, finely chopped
1 teaspoon lime zest
1 teaspoon lime juice
2 teaspoons olive oil
salt and freshly ground black pepper

Pesto does not always have to be made with basil and pine nuts—this variation uses pistachios and parsley for a change. Skin the cucumber if you prefer.

1 Arrange the cucumber, radish, and avocado in a bowl. Sprinkle with salt and pepper, and squeeze the lime juice over the avocado.

2 To make the pesto, combine the parsley with the pistachios, lime zest, lime juice, and olive oil, then sprinkle with salt and pepper. Dollop the pistachio pesto over the vegetables.

Smoothie with Cucumber, Blueberries, Coconut Milk & Mint

Per portion: 257 calories, 3g protein, 23g fat, 9.5g carbohydrate, 4g fiber | Keto factor: 85

SERVES 1
Prep: 10 minutes

½ cup full-fat coconut milk
½ medium (4½ ounces) cucumber, coarsely chopped
1 cup iceberg lettuce leaves or baby spinach, coarsely chopped
½ cup blueberries
2 stems fresh mint, leaves picked

1 Pour the coconut milk and ½ cup of water into a blender.

2 Add the cucumber, lettuce, berries, and mint leaves to the blender and mix at the highest speed until creamy. Pour the smoothie into a large glass.

Want more fiber?
Place 1 tablespoon of chia seeds in a bowl, pour in about ⅓ cup of water, and let the seeds swell for 30 minutes, or overnight. Add this chia pudding to the blender or stir into the smoothie at the end. This results in 324 calories, 6g protein, 27g fat, 10g carbohydrate, and 9.5g fiber per portion (Keto factor: 75).

Smoothie with Spinach, Avocado, Zucchini & Ginger

Per portion: 237 calories, 5g protein, 22g fat, 4g carbohydrate, 6g fiber | Keto factor: 81

SERVES 1
Prep: 10 minutes

½ avocado
3 teaspoons lime juice
⅔ cup baby spinach, with stems
1 small (3½ ounces) zucchini, chopped
1 hazelnut
1 inch piece of fresh ginger, peeled and coarsely chopped
6 teaspoons full-fat coconut milk
1 to 2 pinches of cayenne pepper
salt

1 Remove the flesh from the avocado using a spoon and add with the lime juice to a blender.

2 Add the spinach, zucchini, hazelnut, ginger, and coconut milk with 1 cup of cold water to the avocado in the blender and mix on the highest speed to make a creamy smoothie.

3 Add the cayenne pepper, season with a little salt, and mix in a little water if desired. Pour the smoothie into a large glass.

Keto High-Fiber Bread with Quark & Almonds

Per slice: 133 calories, 7g protein, 10g fat, 1g carbohydrate, 5.5g fiber | Keto factor: 70

MAKES 1 LOAF
Prep: 10 minutes
Baking: 1 hour 20 minutes

1¼ cups quark (40% fat) or
    full-fat cream cheese
3 large eggs
3 teaspoons apple cider vinegar
⅔ cup flaxseed or 1 cup flaxseed
    meal
1 cup almond meal
6 tablespoons psyllium fiber powder
1½ tablespoons gluten-free
    baking powder
1 teaspoon salt
⅔ cup shelled hemp seeds

This is a power bread, miles away from your gluten-heavy loaf; it will keep for a few days, too. Great for a snack loaded with other fibers. See pages 70 and 71 for ideas for toppings.

1 Preheat the oven to 350°F, adding a baking dish filled with water. Line a 4 x 9½-inch loaf pan with parchment paper.

2 Put the quark or cream cheese, eggs, and apple cider vinegar in a bowl and stir until smooth with a hand mixer.

3 Grind the flaxseeds, if using, relatively finely in a spice grinder, mortar and pestle, or blender and put them into a bowl. Add the almond meal, psyllium fiber powder, baking powder, and salt and mix well. Finally, stir in the hemp seeds.

4 Pour the flaxseed mixture into the quark mixture while stirring, then knead the somewhat lumpy dough with your hands and press firmly into the loaf pan.

5 Smooth the top with a damp spatula, score several times diagonally, and bake for 70 minutes. After half the baking time, turn the pan once so that the bread bakes evenly.

6 Insert a skewer to test if the bread is cooked through, then let the bread bake for another 10 minutes with the oven off and the oven door half open.

7 Take out the pan and let the loaf cool completely on a wire rack, and only then cut open.

Tip
Cut the bread into slices, freeze between pieces of parchment paper, and place in a sealable container. You can then take out the bread in slices and toast whenever you need it.

Keto High-Fiber Crispbread

Per crispbread: 47 calories, 2g protein, 4g fat, 0.2g carbohydrate, 3g fiber | Keto factor: 74

MAKES 16 CRISPBREADS
Prep: 15 minutes
Chia: 10 minutes
Baking: 40 minutes
Cooling: approx. 30 minutes

½ cup flaxseed or ¾ cup
   flaxseed meal
1 tablespoon chia seeds
3½ teaspoons poppy seeds
4 teaspoons shelled hemp seeds
3 teaspoons psyllium fiber powder
¼ cup unsweetened
   shredded coconut
½ teaspoon salt
3 teaspoons cold-pressed
   coconut oil

These Scandinavian crispbreads are loaded up with good secret things like chia, hemp, and coconut.

1 Coarsely grind the flaxseeds, if using, in a spice grinder, blender or using a mortar and pestle and put them into a bowl.

2 Add the chia seeds, poppy seeds, hemp, psyllium fiber powder, shredded coconut, and salt. Pour in ⅔ cup of lukewarm water, stir well, and let swell for 10 minutes. Knead in the oil with your hands.

3 Preheat the oven to 350°F. Line a baking sheet with a silicone baking mat or parchment paper.

4 Place the dough in the middle of the mat or paper, cover it with plastic wrap, and roll it out as evenly as possible, leaving a good ½ inch free toward the edge of the baking sheet.

5 Remove the plastic wrap. Quarter the dough sheet by pressing in dividing lines deeply with a knife, then quarter each quarter again so you get sixteen pieces.

6 Bake on the middle shelf for 40 minutes, using a cooking spoon to keep the oven door slightly open. After half the baking time, turn the baking sheet so that the crispbread bakes evenly. Switch off the oven and let the baked crispbread cool slowly in the oven for about 30 minutes. Take out, break apart along the lines, and let the crispbreads cool completely on a wire rack. Store in a container.

Avocado, Pecan & Chive Spread

Per portion: 450 calories, 6g protein, 47g fat, 2g carbohydrate, 9g fiber | Keto factor: 93

SERVES 1
Prep: 10 minutes

⅓ cup pecans
½ large avocado
2 teaspoons lemon juice
½ teaspoon grated lemon zest
salt and freshly ground black pepper
½ small bunch fresh chives,
    finely sliced

Pecans give this spread its own wholesome flavor, but you can use it as a base for other things like flaxseeds or even as a sauce for lunch.

1 Finely grind the pecans in a spice grinder or mortar and pestle.

2 Remove the flesh from the avocado using a spoon and coarsely cut it into pieces. Add to the pecans and make into a creamy paste.

3 Put the avocado mixture into a bowl, add the lemon juice and lemon zest, season with salt and pepper, and mix.

4 Mix three-quarters of the chives into the spread and sprinkle the remaining chives on top as a garnish.

Want more fiber?
When preparing the spread, add 1 tablespoon brown or golden flaxseed with the pecans to the spice grinder or mortar and pestle and grind them together. Then continue as described above. This results in 497 calories, 8g protein, 50g fat, 2g carbohydrate, and 12.5g fiber (Keto factor: 90).

Tip
For a small lunch or dinner, dilute the spread with a little vegetable broth and mix it into 7 ounces of cooked zucchini "noodles." This results in 491 calories, 10g protein, 47g fat, 7g carbohydrate, and 11.5g fiber (Keto factor: 87).

Sesame & Celery Root Spread

Per portion: 382 calories, 8g protein, 36g fat, 7.5g carbohydrate, 8.5g fiber | Keto factor: 85

SERVES 1
Prep: 15 minutes

1 tablespoon peanut oil
½ small (7 ounces) celery root,
    peeled and finely grated
1½ tablespoons sesame seeds
3½ tablespoons full-fat cream cheese
2 teaspoons lemon juice
½ teaspoon grated lemon zest
1 small bunch fresh flat-leaf parsley,
    leaves finely chopped
1 to 2 pinches of cayenne pepper
salt and freshly ground black pepper

1 Heat the oil in a pan and gently fry the celery root for 4 to 5 minutes, stirring regularly. It should not take on any color but be soft and still somewhat firm to the bite. Let cool.

2 In the meantime, roast the sesame seeds in a pan until golden and then let cool.

3 Put the celery root into a bowl and stir in the cream cheese. Mix in the lemon juice and lemon zest with the sesame seeds and parsley. Stir in the cayenne pepper and season with salt and pepper.

Macadamia Arugula Spread

Per portion: 345 calories, 6g protein, 34g fat, 2g carbohydrate, 9.5g fiber | Keto factor: 89

SERVES 1
Prep: 10 minutes

1 cup arugula, coarsely chopped
¼ cup roasted and salted
    macadamia nuts
½ small avocado
2 teaspoons lime juice
1½ teaspoons flaxseed meal
1 to 2 pinches of cayenne pepper
salt and freshly ground black pepper

1 Coarsely chop the arugula and macadamia nuts in a blender or food processor.

2 Remove the flesh from the avocado using a spoon, coarsely dice, and drizzle with the lime juice. Mix with the flaxseed meal, arugula, and macadamia nuts.

3 Finally, stir in the cayenne pepper and season the spread with salt and pepper.

High-Fiber Sandwich Bread

Per portion: 116 calories, 7g protein, 10g fat, 1g carbohydrate, 6g fiber | Keto factor: 78

MAKES 4 SLICES
Prep: 15 minutes
Baking: 40 minutes

2 tablespoons coconut flour
2 tablespoons psyllium fiber powder
1 teaspoon gluten-free
    baking powder
½ teaspoon salt
3 large eggs
1 teaspoon apple cider vinegar
1 tablespoon peanut oil
2 tablespoons sparkling
    mineral water
1½ teaspoons poppy or
    sesame seeds

Use this poppy, psyllium, and coconut bread as a base for any kind of protein topping—rare beef, smoked salmon, ham and tomatoes, smoked mackerel, or even bacon and eggs.

1 Preheat the oven to 300°F, circulating air, and line a 5½ x 8½-inch rectangular baking dish with parchment paper.

2 Mix together the coconut flour, psyllium fiber powder, baking powder, and salt.

3 Separate the eggs and beat the egg whites until stiff. Place the egg yolks in a bowl with the vinegar, peanut oil, and mineral water and whisk with a hand mixer.

4 Stir the coconut flour mixture into the yolks, then add half of the egg whites and stir. Finally, loosely fold in the remaining egg whites.

5 Pour the mixture into the prepared pan and smooth it down with a spatula. Deeply mark four equal pieces with a knife and sprinkle with poppy or sesame seeds.

6 Bake in the oven on the middle shelf for 30 minutes, turning once after half the cooking time so that the bread bakes evenly. Insert a skewer to test if the bread is cooked through, then let cook for another 10 minutes with the oven off and the oven door half open.

7 Take out, cut the sandwich bread in half, put it on a wire rack, and let cool completely.

8 Halve the pieces horizontally and toast as desired, or use in one of the following recipes, toasting beforehand as desired.

Sauerkraut, Mustard Mayonnaise & Pastrami Sandwich

Per portion: 423 calories, 20g protein, 37g fat, 4.5g carbohydrate, 7g fiber | Keto factor: 79

SERVES 1
Prep: 5 minutes

1 slice of High-Fiber Sandwich Bread
    (page 69)
1½ tablespoons full-fat mayonnaise
2 tablespoons full-fat cream cheese
1 teaspoon Dijon mustard
salt and freshly ground black pepper
¼ cup sauerkraut from a jar, drained
2 wafer-thin slices (1¾ ounces)
    of pastrami

The Hi-Fiber sandwich bread on the previous page is fantastic to use for making open sandwiches. Try smoked fish, tomato, basil or ham (see photo on page 68) or this sauerkraut and pastrami version.

1 Halve the sandwich bread horizontally and toast as desired.

2 Mix the mayonnaise with the cream cheese and mustard and season with salt and pepper. Loosen the sauerkraut, cut it into small pieces, add it to the mustard mayonnaise, and mix.

3 Spread the mix on the sandwich halves and loosely place the pastrami slices on top.

See photo on page 68

Chile-Mayonnaise, Lettuce & Egg Sandwich

Per portion: 425 calories, 16g protein, 39g fat, 4g carbohydrate, 6g fiber | Keto factor: 83

SERVES 1
Prep: 10 minutes

1 medium egg
1½ tablespoons full-fat mayonnaise
2 tablespoons full-fat cream cheese
1 teaspoon tomato paste
1 teaspoon sambal oelek
salt and freshly ground black pepper
2 to 3 lettuce leaves
1 slice of High-Fiber Sandwich Bread
    (page 69)

1 Cook the eggs for 5 to 7 minutes until just hard-boiled. Drain, then peel and halve.

2 Mix the mayonnaise with the cream cheese, tomato paste, and sambal oelek, then season with salt and pepper.

3 Halve the sandwich bread horizontally and toast as desired.

4 Spread the chile-mayonnaise on the sandwich halves, add the lettuce, and egg, then season again with salt and pepper.

See photo on page 68

Avocado, Wasabi & Smoked Salmon Sandwich

Per portion: 412 calories, 23g protein, 35g fat, 2g carbohydrate, 10g fiber | Keto factor: 83

SERVES 1

Prep: 5 minutes

½ avocado
1 teaspoon lime juice
1 teaspoon wasabi from a tube
salt and freshly ground black pepper
1 slice High-Fiber Sandwich Bread
   (page 69)
2 slices (1¾ ounces) of
   smoked salmon
1 stem fresh dill, leaves chopped

Wasabi—Japanese horseradish—gives you a little taste of Tokyo to upgrade this classic mix.

1 Remove the flesh from the avocado using a spoon and crush it with a fork. Add the lime juice and wasabi with a little salt and pepper and mix together.

2 Halve the bread horizontally and toast as desired.

3 Brush with the avocado cream and arrange the salmon on top. Season with pepper and sprinkle with the dill.

See photo on page 68

Ham Salad with Gherkins

Per portion: 465 calories, 24g protein, 37g fat, 8g carbohydrate, 6g fiber | Keto factor: 72

SERVES 1
Prep: 15 minutes

¼ cup full-fat cream cheese
2 tablespoons full-fat mayonnaise
1½ teaspoons inulin
salt and freshly ground black pepper
⅓ cup small gherkins, thinly sliced
4 thin slices (3½ ounces) of cooked
    ham, cut into cubes
1 small bunch fresh flat-leaf parsley,
    finely chopped
½ small bunch fresh chives,
    thinly sliced

1 Mix the cream cheese with the mayonnaise and inulin in a bowl. Stir until smooth and season with salt and pepper.

2 Add the gherkins and mix, then top the salad with the ham, parsley, and chives.

Tomato, Avocado & Mozzarella Salad with Almond Pesto

Per portion: 625 calories, 23g protein, 56g fat, 7g carbohydrate, 9.5g fiber | Keto factor: 81

SERVES 1
Prep: 15 minutes

FOR THE PESTO
¼ cup flaked almonds
½ bunch fresh basil
1 to 2 garlic cloves, peeled and
    roughly chopped
2 teaspoons olive oil
salt and freshly ground black pepper

FOR THE SALAD
½ large avocado, cut into cubes
½ cup mini mozzarella balls, sliced
⅔ cup cherry tomatoes, halved
salt and freshly ground black pepper

1 To make the pesto, toast the almonds in a pan until golden, then set aside to cool. Meanwhile, set the basil leaves aside and roughly chop the rest of the basil.

2 Blend the almonds, chopped basil stems, and garlic in a spice ginder, mortar and pestle, or blender to a rough paste. Work in the oil and season the pesto with salt and pepper.

3 To make the salad, put the avocado cubes into a bowl, mix with the mozzarella and tomatoes, and season with salt and pepper.

4 Dollop the almond pesto over the salad and sprinkle with the basil leaves.

Asparagus & Avocado Salad with Peanuts, Chile & Cilantro

Per portion: 457 calories, 11g protein, 43g fat, 7g carbohydrate, 10g fiber | Keto factor: 85

SERVES 1

Prep: 15 minutes

9 to 10 ounces asparagus
3 teaspoons peanut oil
salt and freshly ground black pepper
2 teaspoons lime juice
½ small red chile pepper,
    finely chopped
½ bunch fresh cilantro, stems
    finely chopped and leaves
    coarsely chopped
½ large avocado
¼ cup chopped roasted and
    salted peanuts

Peanuts often star in Thai dishes like this variation. In fact, ¾ cup of peanuts equals 26g of protein. The cilantro and lime freshen the whole thing up.

1 Add about 2 inches salted water to a saucepan and bring to a boil. Insert a steaming basket so that it does not touch the water.

2 Peel the lower third of the asparagus and cut away the woody ends. Detach the tips and cut the stalks into bite-size pieces.

3 First put the thicker pieces of asparagus into the steamer basket and steam for 1 minute, then add the thinner pieces and steam for 1 minute. Finally, add the asparagus tips and steam for 3 to 4 minutes until the asparagus is just cooked. Plunge into ice water and then drain.

4 Put the asparagus pieces into a bowl. Mix the peanut oil with salt, pepper, and 1 teaspoon of the lime juice and pour over the asparagus. Mix in the chile and cilantro stems.

5 Remove the flesh from the avocado using a spoon and dice. Drizzle with the remaining lime juice. Season with salt and pepper and fold into the asparagus. Sprinkle the salad with the chopped cilantro leaves and peanuts.

Spicy Egg Salad

Per portion: 444 calories, 18g protein, 35g fat, 9.5g carbohydrate, 6.5g fiber | Keto factor: 81

SERVES 1

Prep: 15 minutes

2 large eggs
⅓ cup full-fat plain Greek yogurt
1½ tablespoons full-fat mayonnaise
1½ teaspoons inulin
1 teaspoon Dijon mustard
2 teaspoons tomato paste
½ teaspoon paprika
1 to 2 pinches of cayenne pepper
salt and freshly ground black pepper
1 tablespoon mixed fresh or
    frozen herbs
1 teaspoon capers, salted if possible,
    chopped
1 scallion, sliced
⅓ cup cherry tomatoes, quartered

It's the spicing here that does the trick—a little cayenne and paprika, plus the secret ingredient inulin, a probiotic that stimulates the digestive tract.

1 Cook the eggs for 10 minutes, then rinse under cold water, peel, and quarter.

2 In the meantime, stir the yogurt with the mayonnaise, inulin, mustard, and tomato paste until smooth.

3 Add the paprika and cayenne pepper and season with salt and pepper. Stir in the herbs and fold the capers and scallion into the yogurt mixture.

4 Lightly season the tomatoes and egg quarters with salt and pepper, then carefully fold in as well.

Parsnip & Coconut Soup with Curry

Per person: 347 calories, 5g protein, 32g fat, 9g carbohydrate, 8.5g fiber | Keto factor: 83

SERVES 1

Prep: 20 minutes

1 tablespoon cold-pressed
    coconut oil
1 to 2 shallots, finely chopped
1 large (7 ounces) parsnip, peeled
    and diced into 1-inch cubes
½ to 1 teaspoon curry powder
1½ cups gluten-free vegetable broth,
    plus a bit more if needed
⅓ cup full-fat coconut milk
1½ teaspoons inulin
salt and freshly ground black pepper
1 to 2 pinches of red pepper flakes
3 to 4 sprigs fresh cilantro, chopped

A really quick, nourishing soup that you can rustle up from mostly pantry ingredients. Or, if you're super organized, you could make your own homemade broth.

1 Heat the coconut oil in a saucepan and cook the shallots over medium heat until translucent. Add the parsnips and simmer for 1 to 2 minutes while stirring. Sprinkle in the curry powder and stir.

2 Add the broth and 3½ tablespoons of the coconut milk. Bring to a boil, cover, and simmer for 7 minutes until the parsnips are soft.

3 Stir the inulin into the soup and purée the mixture with a hand blender. Depending on the desired consistency, add some more broth or water. Season with salt and pepper.

4 Pour the soup into a deep dish or a bowl and spiral in the remaining coconut milk. Sprinkle with red pepper flakes and the chopped cilantro.

Spinach Soup with Parmesan

Per portion: 407 calories, 17g protein, 34g fat, 5.5g carbohydrate, 6g fiber | Keto factor: 75

SERVES 1
Prep: 10 minutes

1 tablespoon olive oil
1 to 2 shallots, finely chopped
1 to 2 garlic cloves, finely chopped
1¼ cups frozen spinach
1 cup gluten-free vegetable broth,
    plus a bit more if needed
3½ tablespoons full-fat
    cream cheese
¼ cup freshly grated Parmesan (or
    an alternative vegetarian hard
    cheese)
pinch of freshly grated nutmeg
salt and freshly ground black pepper

Another fast soup from pantry and freezer ingredients that you can buy ahead and just keep on hand.

1 Heat the oil in a saucepan and cook the shallots over medium heat until translucent. Add the garlic and sauté briefly. Add the frozen spinach, stir, and pour over the broth. Bring to a boil, stirring until the spinach has thawed, then simmer for another 2 minutes.

2 Stir in the cream cheese and Parmesan and add a little more broth if needed. Season with the nutmeg, salt, and pepper. Purée the soup in a blender until the spinach is finely chopped. Pour the soup into a deep dish or a bowl to serve.

Want more fiber?
Mix 3 teaspoons inulin into the soup. That will be 419 calories, 17g protein, 34g fat, 6.5g carbohydrate, and 15g fiber per person (Keto factor: 73).

See photo on page 79

Radish "Fries" with Egg & Flax-Shallots

Per portion: 421 calories, 20g protein, 34g fat, 8.5g carbohydrate, 9g fiber | Keto factor: 73

SERVES 1
Prep: 15 minutes

½ small (7¾ ounces) daikon radish
4 teaspoons cold-pressed
    coconut oil
salt and freshly ground black pepper
½ to 1 teaspoon smoked or
    sweet paprika
2 to 3 shallots, finely diced
3 teaspoons freshly crushed flaxseed
    or flaxseed meal
2 large eggs
4 to 5 chives, sliced

Eggs are great once or twice a week, but here I have paired them with hidden flaxseeds, which pack a lot of fiber, so use generously. The coconut oil balances them out.

1 Peel the radish, pat dry, cut into ½-inch slices, and pat dry again.

2 Heat 3 teaspoons of the coconut oil in a large pan. Place the radish slices next to each other and fry for 5 to 6 minutes until golden brown, turning several times. Season with salt and pepper and dust with the paprika.

3 Push the radishes to the edge, put the shallots into the middle of the pan, and braise over low heat. Sprinkle the flaxseed over the shallots, mix well, and gently fry, then season with some salt and pepper.

4 At the same time, heat the remaining 1 teaspoon coconut oil in another pan, break in the eggs, and fry over medium heat.

5 Put the radishes on a plate and spread the flaxseed-shallot mixture over them. Put the fried eggs on top, season with salt and pepper, and sprinkle with the chives.

See photo on page 83

Mediterranean Celery Root with Feta Cheese, Olives & Pumpkin Seeds

Per portion: 555 calories, 18g protein, 50g fat, 7g carbohydrate, 10g fiber | Keto factor: 81

SERVES 1

Prep: 25 minutes

3 tablespoons olive oil
¼ celery root, peeled and diced
salt and freshly ground black pepper
3½ teaspoons pumpkin seeds
12 coarsely chopped pitted
    black olives
½ cup full-fat crumbled feta
5 to 6 sprigs fresh thyme,
    leaves chopped
1 to 2 pinches of red pepper flakes

Celery root is an underrated vegetable, though a bit messy in the kitchen; it's best to just carve away the skin with a big, heavy knife and give yourself a neat square to work with. Here I have diced it into cubes and given it some spiky flavors to surprise.

1 Heat the oil in a pan and fry the celery root gently over medium heat for 2 to 3 minutes, without changing color. Season with salt, put on the lid, and cook over very low heat for 15 minutes, stirring occasionally.

2 In the meantime, roast the pumpkin seeds in a pan.

3 Add a generous amount of pepper to the cooked celery root and put it on a plate. Spread the olives, crumbled feta, and pumpkin seeds on top and sprinkle with thyme and red pepper flakes. Serve hot or lukewarm.

Kale & Cheese Omelet

Per portion: 466 calories, 25g protein, 37g fat, 5.5g carbohydrate, 8.5g fiber | Keto factor: 71

SERVES 1
Prep: 15 minutes

1½ tablespoons butter
1 to 2 shallots, finely diced
½ cup chopped frozen kale
2 large eggs
1 to 2 pinches of cayenne pepper
pinch of freshly grated nutmeg
salt and freshly ground black pepper
3 teaspoons potato fibers
    (if available)
⅓ cup grated aged Gouda

1 Heat the butter in a pan and sauté the shallots over medium heat until transparent. Add the frozen kale and sauté for 5 to 6 minutes, stirring occasionally.

2 Whisk the eggs, then stir in the cayenne pepper and nutmeg and season with salt and pepper.

3 Sprinkle the potato fibers, if using, over the kale mixture and mix well. Pour the egg mixture over and let cook for 2 minutes over low heat. Sprinkle the cheese on top, put the lid on, and cook for another 2 to 3 minutes until the egg is sticky but not dry and the cheese has melted.

4 Slide the omelet onto a plate and serve.

Mushroom Scallion Omelet

Per portion: 450 calories, 24g protein, 36g fat, 4.5g carbohydrate, 7g fiber | Keto factor: 72

SERVES 1
Prep: 15 minutes

7 ounces mushrooms
2 to 3 scallions
2 large eggs
salt and freshly ground black pepper
4 teaspoons peanut oil
4 teaspoons freshly crushed brown
    or golden flaxseed
2 teaspoons tamari (gluten-free
    soy sauce)
1 to 2 pinches of red pepper flakes

1 Chop the stems off the mushrooms and cut the caps into ¼-inch slices. Cut the white and green parts of the scallions separately into rings. Whisk the eggs and season with a little salt and pepper.

2 Heat the oil in a pan and stir-fry the mushrooms over high heat for 4 to 5 minutes. Reduce the temperature to low and add the flaxseed with the white scallion rings. Drizzle with the soy sauce and season with pepper.

3 Pour the egg mixture over and let it gently cook for 3 to 4 minutes. Sprinkle the omelet with the green scallion rings and red pepper flakes and serve immediately.

Want more fiber?
Replace the mushrooms with the same amount of oyster mushrooms. This results in 433 calories, 22g protein, 36g fat, 4g carbohydrate, and 13g fiber per portion (Keto factor: 75).

Cauliflower with a Parmesan Almond Crust

Per portion: 518 calories, 21g protein, 44g fat, 7.5g carbohydrate, 10g fiber | Keto factor: 76

SERVES 1

Prep: 20 minutes

½ small cauliflower, cut into florets
2 tablespoons softened butter
½ cup freshly grated Parmesan
   (or an alternative vegetarian hard
   cheese)
¼ cup almond meal
salt and freshly ground black pepper
⅓ cup cherry tomatoes, quartered

Cauliflower can be one of the least expensive and most rewarding vegetables. Its cooking water makes a great vegan broth. You can make this ahead and finish under the broiler when you're ready.

1 Bring a pan of salted water to a boil. Depending on the size of the cauliflower florets, cook for 6 to 7 minutes until just tender, then drain and let the water evaporate a little.

2 In the meantime, spread a small baking dish with a little of the butter. Mix the rest of the butter with the Parmesan and almond meal into a paste, season with salt and pepper, and press flat between two layers of plastic wrap—the layer of paste should be slightly smaller than the baking dish.

3 Preheat the oven to broil. Put the cauliflower in the prepared dish and spread the tomato pieces in between, then season.

4 Peel the plastic wrap off the paste and cover the cauliflower mixture with it.

5 Broil for 4 to 5 minutes until golden brown.

Salmon Fillet on Creamy Kale

Per portion: 591 calories, 33g protein, 47g fat, 8g carbohydrate, 7.5g fiber | Keto factor: 71

SERVES 1
Prep: 20 minutes

An all-in-one-pan dish that you build at your own speed but that has Oscar appeal and minimum cleanup.

FOR THE KALE
3 teaspoons peanut oil
1 to 2 shallots, finely diced
⅔ cup chopped frozen kale
¼ cup gluten-free vegetable broth
3 tablespoons heavy cream
2 tablespoons full-fat cream cheese

FOR THE FISH
4½ ounces salmon fillet
    (without skin)
salt and freshly ground black pepper

1 Heat the oil in a pan and sauté the shallots over medium heat until transparent. Add the frozen kale and braise for 1 minute, stirring. Pour in the broth and cream and bring to a boil.

2 Stir in the cream cheese, put the lid on, and let simmer for about 5 minutes over medium heat.

3 In the meantime, remove any gray fat and bones that may have remained on the salmon. Rinse under cold water and pat dry. Place the salmon on the kale, season with salt and pepper, put the lid on, and let cook for 3 to 5 minutes, depending on the thickness of the fish, until the salmon is tender and slightly glassy. Serve immediately.

Want more fiber?
Mix 1½ teaspoons inulin into the cream cheese before adding to the kale. This results in 597 calories, 33g protein, 47g fat, 8g carbohydrate, and 12g fiber per portion (Keto factor: 71).

Shrimp with Asparagus and Olive & Pistachio Topping

 GF

Per portion: 583 calories, 31g protein, 46g fat, 9g carbohydrate, 10g fiber | Keto factor: 71

SERVES 1
Prep: 20 minutes

9 to 10 ounces asparagus
2 tablespoons olive oil
salt and freshly ground black pepper
squeeze of lemon juice
3½ ounces extra large shrimp

FOR THE TOPPING
1 small bunch fresh flat-leaf parsley,
    coarsely chopped
¼ cup pistachios
2½ teaspoons golden flaxseed
salt and freshly ground black pepper
1 teaspoon grated lemon zest
1 to 2 sprinkles of lemon juice
2 tablespoons coarsely chopped
    pitted green olives

Sometimes just the way you cut vegetables makes a difference. Cutting the asparagus small like beans allows the shrimp to star. Plus the dressing has crunched-down pistachios and coarsely chopped olives for a surprise element.

1 To make the topping, put the parsley into a blender or mortar and pestle with the pistachios and flaxseed and coarsely chop, not too finely. Pour into a bowl, season with salt and pepper, and then stir in the lemon zest and lemon juice. Mix in the olives.

2 Peel the lower third of the asparagus, cut away the woody ends, and cut into bite-size pieces. Heat 1 tablespoon of the oil in a pan and fry the asparagus over medium heat for 5 to 7 minutes until firm and lightly browned. Season with salt, pepper, and lemon juice to taste.

3 As soon as the asparagus starts to fry, heat up the remaining tablespoon of oil in another pan and fry the shrimp for about 4 to 5 minutes on both sides, so that they are rosy on the outside but still glassy on the inside. Season with salt and pepper. Arrange the shrimp on a plate with the asparagus and sprinkle on the topping.

Chicken Broccoli Curry with Coconut Topping

Per person: 612 calories, 35g protein, 48g fat, 8.5g carbohydrate, 9g fiber | Keto factor: 71

SERVES 1

Prep: 20 minutes

Curry always sounds more exotic—and tastes more exotic—than it really is in terms of work for the kitchen. This is my go-to variation where all the theater is in the toppings, but there is depth of flavor here, too.

FOR THE CURRY

5 teaspoons cold-pressed coconut oil
3½ ounces chicken breast, cut
    into strips
salt
1 head broccoli, cut into florets
2 teaspoons tomato paste
1 teaspoon Thai red curry paste
½ cup gluten-free vegetable broth
3½ tablespoons full-fat cream
    cheese

FOR THE TOPPING

1 tablespoon unsweetened
    shredded coconut
1 tablespoon coarsely chopped
    roasted and salted peanuts
½ bunch fresh cilantro, leaves and
    stems chopped

1 For the curry, heat 2 teaspoons of coconut oil in a wok or saucepan, add the chicken strips, and cook over medium to high heat, stirring, for 1½ minutes until golden brown. Season with salt and remove.

2 Add the remaining 3 teaspoons of the coconut oil to the wok or saucepan. Fry the broccoli florets for 1 minute, then push to the edge. Add the tomato paste and curry paste to the center of the wok, roast for a few minutes, and then deglaze with the broth. Mix everything well, then cook the broccoli over medium heat for about 5 minutes.

3 Meanwhile, for the topping, roast the shredded coconut in a small pan until golden.

4 Stir the cream cheese into the broccoli. Add the chicken and cook for 2 minutes. Season with salt.

5 Spoon the curry into a bowl or plate and serve with the shredded coconut, peanuts, and a sprinkle of cilantro.

Lamb Loin with Rosemary & Celery Purée

Per portion: 487 calories, 26g protein, 40g fat, 7g carbohydrate, 10g fiber | Keto factor: 74

SERVES 1

Prep: 25 minutes

FOR THE PURÉE

5 teaspoons olive oil

¼ celery root, peeled and diced

1 to 2 garlic cloves

2 sprigs fresh rosemary

2 tablespoons gluten-free meat or
    vegetable broth or water

2 tablespoons slivered almonds

pinch of freshly grated nutmeg

salt and freshly ground black pepper

FOR THE MEAT

1 teaspoon olive oil

1 large lamb loin or 2 small
    lamb loins, any fat and
    sinew removed

salt and freshly ground black pepper

You cannot beat a roast—but this simplified version is quick and easy to put together and seasoned classically with rosemary and mashed celery root (or potatoes if you prefer, or half and half, as they can go well together).

1 Heat the oil in a large pan. Add the celery root, garlic, and a sprig of rosemary and sauté over medium heat for 2 to 3 minutes, without the celery root taking on any color. Pour in the broth, put the lid on, and cook over low heat for 15 minutes.

2 Remove the lid and cook for 2 minutes until the liquid boils and the celery root is soft. Now strip the leaves from the second rosemary sprig and chop them very finely. Set aside. Toast the slivered almonds until golden in a pan.

3 As soon as the celery root is ready, heat the oil in a pan and sear the lamb all over on medium to high heat, then fry for 2 to 3 minutes depending on the thickness. Remove the lamb from the pan, season with salt and pepper, and let rest for a while. Add 2 teaspoons of water to the pan and mix with the lamb cooking juices.

4 Meanwhile, remove the rosemary sprig from the celery root, add the celery root to a tall mixing bowl, and purée with a hand blender. Add the nutmeg and season with salt and pepper.

5 Arrange the rosemary and celery root purée with the lamb loin on a plate and drizzle over the cooking juices. Sprinkle with the chopped rosemary and slivered almonds.

Want more fiber?

Before puréeing, mix 1½ teaspoons inulin into the celery root. That results in 493 calories, 26g protein, 40g fat, 7g carbohydrate, and 14.5g fiber per person (Keto factor: 73).

Carrot Noodles with Turkey Strips

Per portion: 533 calories, 31g protein, 43g fat, 10g carbohydrate, 8g fiber | Keto factor: 70

SERVES 1
Prep: 15 minutes

2 tablespoons sesame seeds
2 large carrots
3½ ounces turkey scallops
7 teaspoons cold-pressed coconut oil
salt
2 teaspoons tamari (gluten-free
    soy sauce)
1 small bunch fresh cilantro,
    leaves and delicate stems
    coarsely chopped
1 to 2 pinches of red pepper flakes

Cheap, quick, and yet wonderfully aromatic, this stir-fry can be put together in just 15 minutes. That's what I call fast food.

1 Roast the sesame seeds in a pan until golden yellow, then let cool.

2 Peel the carrots and use a spiralizer to turn them into "noodles." Alternatively, slice them into thin strips. Cut the turkey into ½-inch-thick strips across the grain.

3 Heat 3 teaspoons of the coconut oil in a wok or pan. Salt the meat, then sear it in the wok and cook over high heat for 2 minutes, stirring well. Remove and set aside, covered.

4 Heat the remaining coconut oil in the wok and stir-fry the noodles for 3 to 5 minutes, depending on the thickness, over high heat. Add the meat back in and fry for another 2 minutes. Drizzle with the soy sauce and remove from the heat.

5 Transfer to a bowl or onto a plate, sprinkle with the sesame seeds, cilantro, and red pepper flakes, and serve immediately.

Tip
It's best to roast a large amount of sesame seeds and store them in a screwtop jar—they can be kept for several weeks.

Radish Noodles alla Carbonara

Per portion: 598 calories, 31g protein, 48g fat, 10g carbohydrate, 5.5g fiber | Keto factor: 71

SERVES 1

Prep: 20 minutes

½ medium (9½ ounces) daikon
    radish
2 teaspoons peanut or olive oil
1 to 2 shallots, sliced
3 slices (2¾ ounces) cooked ham,
    thinly sliced
3½ tablespoons heavy cream
3½ tablespoons full-fat cream
    cheese
salt and freshly ground black pepper
½ cup freshly grated Parmesan
    (or an alternative vegetarian hard
    cheese)

Normal pasta is all carbs, so here the recipe uses vegetable spirals from a daikon radish, which are great value. It looks like carbonara but tastes wonderfully fresh and different.

1 Peel the daikon radish and use a spiralizer to make "noodles."

2 Heat the oil in a pan and sauté the shallots over medium heat until transparent. Add the ham and fry for 1 minute, then remove from the pan and set aside.

3 Put the radish noodles into the pan and stir-fry over medium heat for 2 minutes, without changing color. Stir in the shallot and ham mixture, pour in the cream, and put the lid on. Depending on the thickness of the noodles, simmer for 3 to 4 minutes until they're done but still have a bit of a bite.

4 Stir in the cream cheese. Season with salt and pepper and sprinkle with the Parmesan.

Want more fiber?

Stir 1½ teaspoons inulin into the cream sauce. That will make 604 calories, 31g protein, 48g fat, 10.5g carbohydrate, and 10g fiber per person (Keto factor: 72).

Phase 2:
Stabilization

At this point, those who want to lose more weight or continue to eat healthily should extend the keto phase. Everyone else is slowly adding carbohydrates again.

Maximum of 50g of carbohydrates
and up to 45g of fiber per day

Morning Bowl with Quark, Raspberries & Almonds

Per person: 418 calories, 18g protein, 33g fat, 7.5g carbohydrate, 13g fiber | Keto factor: 71

SERVES 1
Prep: 5 minutes
Chia: at least 10 minutes (or overnight) soaking

1 tablespoon chia seeds
⅓ cup quark (20% fat) or full-fat cream cheese
2 teaspoons lime juice
3 teaspoons wheatgerm oil
pinch of kosher salt
⅔ cup raspberries
2 tablespoons chopped almonds

Wheatgerm oil is a fabulous source of antioxidants. A little goes a long way in terms of contribution to your daily intake, and mixed with chia and fresh berries, it makes an excellent start to any day.

1 Put the chia seeds into a bowl, pour ½ cup of warm water over them, stir several times, and let them swell for at least 10 minutes. Alternatively, pour the same amount of cold water over them in the evening and let them soak, covered, in the refrigerator overnight.

2 Stir the quark or cream cheese, lime juice, and oil into the chia mixture and add the salt as desired.

3 Spread the raspberries over the quark mixture.

4 Sprinkle the almonds on top.

Morning Bowl with Blueberries & Crunchy Hemp Seeds

Per person: 387 calories, 17g protein, 30g fat, 6.5g carbohydrate, 14g fiber | Keto factor: 70

SERVES 1

Prep: 5 minutes

Chia: at least 10 minutes (or overnight) soaking

1 tablespoon chia seeds

⅓ cup quark (20% fat) or full-fat cream cheese

2 teaspoons lime juice

2 teaspoons wheatgerm oil

pinch of ground cinnamon or 1 teaspoon vanilla extract

3 tablespoons unshelled hemp seeds

½ cup blueberries

I have loaded this breakfast up with other good things like hemp and cinnamon or vanilla, whichever flavor you feel like for the working week.

1 Put the chia seeds into a bowl and pour ⅓ cup of warm water over them. Stir several times and let them soak for at least 10 minutes. Alternatively, pour ½ cup of cold water over them in the evening and let them soak, covered, in the refrigerator overnight.

2 Stir the quark or cream cheese, lime juice, and wheatgerm oil into the chia seeds.

3 Season the mixture with the cinnamon or vanilla extract.

4 Stir half of the hemp seeds into the quark mixture and sprinkle the rest over the top.

5 Adorn with blueberries.

See photo page 102

Morning Bowl with Avocado, Pumpkin Seed Pesto & Raspberries

Per person: 382 calories, 10g protein, 33g fat, 8g carbohydrate, 14g fiber | Keto factor: 78

SERVES 1

Prep: 10 minutes

1 small avocado
2 teaspoons lime juice
3 to 4 sprigs fresh basil
2 tablespoons pumpkin seeds
1 teaspoon grated lime zest
salt and freshly ground
    black pepper
1 cup raspberries

Pumpkin seeds are a great natural laxative passed down to us from Central America. They are also full of good things like magnesium, potassium, and calcium. Basil sets them off beautifully. Pump it up.

1 Remove the flesh of the avocado with a spoon, dice, and put into a bowl. Drizzle with 1 teaspoon of the lime juice.

2 Set some of the basil leaves aside and coarsely chop the rest with the pumpkin seeds, lime zest, and remaining teaspoon of lime juice in a food processor, as you would a traditional pesto.

3 Season with pepper and a pinch of salt and spread the pesto in dollops over the avocado.

4 Arrange the raspberries over the avocado and garnish with the remaining basil leaves.

Tip

For a variation, replace the basil with mint.

See photo page 107

Morning Bowl with Carrot, Avocado & Pumpkin Seeds

Per person: 420 calories, 11g protein, 38g fat, 6g carbohydrate, 16g fiber | Keto factor: 81

SERVES 1

Prep: 10 minutes

1 large carrot, peeled
2 tablespoons crushed golden
    flaxseed or flaxseed meal
1 teaspoon wheatgerm oil
1 to 2 pinches of red pepper flakes
salt and freshly ground black pepper
1 small avocado
2 teaspoons lemon juice
1 tablespoon pumpkin seeds

I have loaded this bowl up with more good things—you interchange and swap as you like through the week. Some red pepper flakes for fire and flax to do yourself some good.

1 Grate the carrot medium coarsely or finely julienne it into a serving bowl.

2 Mix with the flaxseed, wheatgerm oil, red pepper flakes, and a pinch of salt.

3 Remove the flesh of the avocado with a spoon and cut into wedges or cubes.

4 Arrange the avocado over the carrot mixture, drizzle with the lemon juice, and season with salt and pepper.

5 Sprinkle the bowl with the pumpkin seeds.

Kale Smoothie with Avocado, Cucumber & Coconut

Per person: 280 calories, 8g protein, 25g fat, 7g carbohydrate, 13g fiber | Keto factor: 80

SERVES 1
Prep: 5 minutes

½ medium avocado
½ medium (3½ ounces) cucumber, diced
½ bunch fresh flat-leaf parsley, coarsely chopped
½ cup chopped frozen kale
¼ cup unsweetened shredded coconut
⅔ to ¾ cup carbonated mineral water
salt and freshly ground black pepper

Smoothies are a natural ally on the keto diet, as they are quick to prepare and handy to carry around, and can be loaded up with all manner of means to get your five or seven a day.

1 Remove the flesh of the avocado with a spoon and chop into chunks.

2 Put the cucumber, parsley, avocado, frozen kale, and shredded coconut into a blender.

3 Pour ⅔ cup of the mineral water into the mixture and blend on the highest setting until creamy. Depending on your desired consistency, blend in the remaining mineral water.

4 Season with salt and pepper and pour into a large glass.

See photo page 110

Red Pepper Smoothie

Per portion: 332 calories, 12g protein, 27g fat, 7g carbohydrate, 13.5g fiber | Keto factor: 73

SERVES 1
Prep: 10 minutes
Chia: at least 10 minutes (or overnight) soaking

1 tablespoon chia seeds
1 to 2 red bell peppers, chopped
½ red chile pepper, chopped
2 tablespoons almond butter
salt and freshly ground black pepper
3 teaspoons lemon juice
1 teaspoon flaxseed oil

1 Put the chia seeds into a bowl, pour ⅔ cup of warm water over them, stir several times, and let them swell for at least 10 minutes. Alternatively, pour the same amount of cold water over them in the evening and let them soak, covered, in the refrigerator overnight.

2 Put the chia mixture into a blender, then add the red bell peppers, chile pepper, and almond butter and blend on the highest setting.

3 Season with salt and pepper, then incorporate the lemon juice and oil and pour into a large glass.

See photo page 111

Kale Smoothie with Cucumber & Peanut

Per person: 407 calories, 18g protein, 32g fat, 7g carbohydrate, 15.5g fiber | Keto factor: 71

SERVES 1
Prep: 5 minutes

½ medium (3½ ounces) cucumber,
    coarsely chopped
½ cup chopped frozen kale
¼ cup natural or roasted peanuts
2 tablespoons flaxseed
¾ to 1¼ cups carbonated
    mineral water
salt and freshly ground black pepper
1 to 2 pinches of cayenne pepper
1 teaspoon lime juice
1 teaspoon grated lime zest
2 teaspoons flaxseed oil

You can use fresh or frozen kale here. Frozen is useful in that it's ready for when you need it. For fresh, cut the leaves off the steams first—kale stalks are only really good for a broth.

1 Add the cucumber, frozen kale, peanuts, flaxseed, and ¾ cup of the mineral water into the blender and mix until creamy.

2 Depending on the desired consistency, add the remaining mineral water and season with salt and pepper.

3 Add the cayenne pepper, lime juice, lime zest, and flaxseed oil and mix again.

4 Pour the smoothie into a large glass.

See photo page 111

Overnight Chia Muesli with Coconut & Hemp Seeds

Per person: 428 calories, 13g protein, 36g fat, 7.5g carbohydrate, 16.5g fiber | Keto factor: 76

SERVES 1
Prep: 10 minutes
Chia: overnight soaking

2 tablespoons chia seeds
3 tablespoons shelled hemp seeds
¼ cup unsweetened shredded
    coconut
3½ tablespoons full-fat
    coconut milk
pinch of salt
2 teaspoons lime juice
pinch of ground cardamom
ground cinnamon, to taste
⅔ cup raspberries or blueberries

1 Mix the chia seeds, hemp seeds, and shredded coconut in a bowl. Stir in 1 cup of warm water and let soak for at least 10 minutes. Stir again, cover, and let soak in the refrigerator overnight.

2 The next morning, mix with the coconut milk, salt, and lime juice, and sprinkle the spices over the top.

3 Spread the berries over the mixture.

Overnight Chia Muesli with Blueberries

Per person: 419 calories, 18g protein, 33g fat, 8g carbohydrate, 15g fiber | Keto factor: 71

SERVES 1
Prep: 5 minutes
Chia: overnight soaking

2 tablespoons chia seeds
1 tablespoon shelled hemp seeds
¼ cup unsweetened shredded
    coconut
⅓ cup quark (20% fat) or full-fat
    cream cheese
pinch of salt
1 to 2 teaspoons lime juice
pinch of ground cardamom
ground cinnamon, to taste
1 teaspoon wheatgerm oil
½ cup blueberries

1 Mix the chia seeds, hemp seeds, and shredded coconut in a bowl. Stir in 1 cup of warm water and let soak for at least 10 minutes. Stir again, cover, and let soak in the refrigerator overnight.

2 The next morning, mix with the quark or cream cheese, salt, and lime juice, and sprinkle the spices over the top.

3 Drizzle with wheatgerm oil.

4 Spread the blueberries over the muesli.

Tip
Try a variation with cocoa: sprinkle the muesli with 1 teaspoon dark unsweetened cocoa after tasting.

Nutty Topping with Cacao Nibs

Per portion (1oz): 140 calories, 3.5g protein, 13g fat, 2.5g carbohydrate, 4g fiber | Keto factor: 85

MAKES 1 JAR
Prep: 10 minutes

⅓ cup unsweetened
    shredded coconut
¼ cup pecans
¼ cup pistachios
¼ cup cacao nibs

1 Toast the coconut in a pan, then take it off the heat and let it cool.

2 Crush the pecans between your fingers, then add with the pistachios and cacao nibs to a spice grinder, mortar and pestle, or blender and mix briefly. The mixture should not be too fine.

3 In a bowl, mix together the coconut, nuts, and cacao nibs. The topping can be stored in an airtight jar and should be consumed within 1 to 2 months.

Topping with Mixed Seeds

Per portion (1oz): 123 calories, 6g protein, 10g fat, 1g carbohydrate, 6g fiber | Keto factor: 71

MAKES 1 JAR
Prep: 5 minutes

3 tablespoons shelled hemp seeds
¼ cup flaxseed
2½ tablespoons poppy seeds
2 ½ tablespoons sesame seeds

This topping would go well with any of the morning bowls in this book. It is also used in the Asparagus with High-Fiber Topping recipe (see page 147) and is great with vegetable dishes.

1 Grind the hemp seeds in a spice grinder, mortar and pestle, or blender as finely as possible, then add the flaxseed and chop. Put into a bowl and mix in the poppy and sesame seeds. The topping can be stored in an airtight jar and should be consumed within 1 to 2 months.

Spicy Coconut Topping

Per portion (1oz): 125 calories, 5g protein, 10g fat, 1g carbohydrate, 7g fiber | Keto factor: 74

MAKES 1 JAR
Prep: 10 minutes

½ cup unsweetened shredded
    coconut
3 tablespoons shelled hemp seeds
¼ cup golded flaxseed
1 teaspoon salt
1 teaspoon red pepper flakes

This topping goes with all the smoothies, vegetable dishes, and salads in this book, as well as pure avocado.

1 Toast the coconut in a pan, then take it off the heat and let it cool. Crush the hemp seeds in a spice grinder, mortar and pestle, or blender as finely as possible. Add the flaxseed and mix again. Put in a bowl with the coconut, salt, and pepper flakes and mix together.

2 Keep stored in an airtight jar and consume within 1 to 2 months.

Keto High-Fiber Nut Bread

Per slice (1½oz): 136 calories, 5g protein, 11g fat, 1g carbohydrate, 7.5g fiber | Keto factor: 72

**MAKES 1 LOAF
(ABOUT 1 POUND 13
OUNCES)**

Prep: 10 minutes
Soaking: at least 10 minutes
Baking: 1½ to 1¾ hours

¼ cup chia seeds
1 tablespoon apple cider vinegar
1 cup flaxseed meal
5 tablespoons psyllium
    fiber powder
1 teaspoon salt
1½ tablespoons gluten-free
    baking powder
⅔ cup pecans
1¼ cups slivered almonds
⅓ cup pumpkin seeds
⅓ cup sunflower seeds
⅓ cup freshly crushed
    brown flaxseed
2 tablespoons walnut oil

You can have an enjoyable 10 minutes getting your hands dirty with this great loaf dense with seeds and nuts. Then just let the oven do its work while you put your feet up. This bread is a perfect addition to the soups and salads in this book and, of course, also tastes great for breakfast, lunch, or dinner.

1 Mix the chia seeds in a bowl with the vinegar and 1¼ cups of warm water, stir thoroughly, and let soak for at least 10 minutes, stirring occasionally.

2 In the meantime, preheat the oven to 350°F and line a 1-pound loaf pan with parchment paper.

3 Mix the flaxseed meal, psyllium fiber powder, and salt in a bowl. Sift the baking powder over it and mix together.

4 Crush the pecans and add with the almonds, pumpkin seeds, sunflower seeds, and flaxseed and mix together.

5 Add the soaked chia seeds and process everything in a mixer with the dough hook attachment. Knead again with your hands and work in the oil.

6 Pour the mixture into the prepared pan, press down well, smooth the surface with a spatula, and score several times at an angle.

7 Bake for 80 to 90 minutes. Turn off the oven and leave the bread in the oven for another 10 to 15 minutes.

8 Lift the bread out of the pan and let cool completely on a wire rack.

Tip
To store the bread, cut into thin slices, as the bread is very rich and filling. Place in an airtight container between pieces of parchment paper and freeze.

Basic Crepes

Per person: 299 calories, 13g protein, 25g fat, 2g carbohydrate, 9.5g fiber | Keto factor: 75

SERVES 1

Prep: 10 minutes

1 large egg
2 tablespoons full-fat cream cheese
3½ teaspoons flaxseed meal
1½ teaspoons inulin
pinch of salt
2 teaspoons cold-pressed coconut oil

Crepes are far too good to save for the weekend. And they make a great meal at any time of the day with different toppings or fillings. Let your imagination run wild.

1 Whisk the egg and cream cheese in a bowl until smooth, then work in 6 teaspoons of water. Add the flaxseed meal, inulin, and a pinch of salt, stir, and let it rest briefly until the dough gets to a somewhat oatmeal-like consistency.

2 Brush 1 teaspoon of the the oil over a large, nonstick skillet. Add the batter, and with a silicone spatula, spread to the edge of the pan. Cook for about 1 minute over medium heat, then slide onto a large plate.

3 Heat the remaining teaspoon of oil, turn the crepe, and then slide it back into the pan and cook the other side for 1 minute. Then, with occasional turning, cook for another 3 minutes.

4 Slide the crepe out of the pan onto a plate and combine with a topping of your choice (see the following recipes). Eat warm or cold.

See photo page 120

Crepes with Spicy Cheese & Sprouts

Per person: 513 calories, 30g protein, 41g fat, 2g carbohydrate, 10g fiber | Keto factor: 72

SERVES 1

Prep: 15 minutes

¾ cup coarsely chopped Gouda
2 pinches of red pepper flakes
handful of alfalfa sprouts

1 Prepare the crepe as described above and place in a skillet.

2 Spread the Gouda over the crepe and sprinkle with the red pepper flakes. Put on the lid and let the cheese melt.

3 Sprinkle the sprouts over the crepe. Serve immediately.

See photo page 120

Breakfast Crepes with Vanilla Yogurt & Berries

Per person: 437 calories, 16g protein, 35g fat, 8g carbohydrate, 16.5g fiber | Keto factor: 72

SERVES 1
Prep: 15 minutes

½ cup full-fat plain Greek yogurt
1½ tablespoons vanilla extract
½ cup blueberries
5 small fresh mint leaves

1 Prepare the crepe as described at left and place on a plate.

2 Mix the yogurt with the vanilla extract and distribute over the crepe. Sprinkle the blueberries and mint over the top.

See photo page 121

Crepes with Avocado & Carrot Filling

Per person: 433 calories, 15g protein, 41g fat, 4.5g carbohydrate, 15g fiber | Keto factor: 81

SERVES 1
Prep: 15 minutes

½ avocado
salt and freshly ground black pepper
1 to 2 pinches of red pepper flakes
1 teaspoon lime juice
1 small carrot, peeled and grated
2 fresh parsley stems, coarsely
   chopped

1 Prepare the crepe as described at left and place on a plate.

2 Remove the flesh of the avocado with a spoon, crush with a fork, and season with salt, pepper, and the red pepper flakes. Mix with the lime juice and spoon onto the crepe.

3 Distribute the carrot over the avocado mixture, then sprinkle the parsley over the top.

4 Roll the crepe up into a wrap and serve.

See photo page 121

Mushroom Cream with Flaxseed & Pumpkin Seeds

Per person: 342 calories, 20g protein, 28g fat, 3.5g carbohydrate, 14.5g fiber | Keto factor: 74

SERVES 1

Prep: 15 minutes

2 teaspoons peanut oil

7 ounces button mushrooms, diced

salt and freshly ground black pepper

2 tablespoons brown or
  golden flaxseed

¼ cup pumpkin seeds

½ large bunch fresh flat-leaf parsley,
  coarsely chopped

2 teaspoons lemon juice

1 teaspoon grated lemon zest

This is my great standby: it can go on toast, as a filling for zucchini or bell peppers, in a crepe, or just as a side with grilled meat—plus it has hidden benefits with the flax and pumpkin seeds.

1 Heat the peanut oil in a pan and cook the mushrooms over high heat for about 4 minutes, stirring frequently, until the liquid has almost evaporated. Remove from the heat and season with salt and pepper.

2 Finely grind the flaxseed and pumpkin seeds in a food processor. Add the parsley and mushrooms and grind again.

3 Stir the lemon juice and lemon zest into the mushroom cream and season again with salt and pepper.

Tip

This spread goes well with the savory breads and crepes in this book and should be stored in the refrigerator and consumed within 1 to 2 days.

Chanterelle Pesto

Per serving: 335 calories, 14g protein, 30g fat, 4g carbohydrate, 13g fiber | Keto factor: 79

SERVES 1

Prep: 20 minutes

1 tablespoon canola oil

9 ounces chanterelle or other firm
   wild mushrooms, diced

1 to 2 shallots, coarsely chopped

1 small bunch fresh flat-leaf parsley

¼ cup almonds, chopped

¼ cup freshly grated Parmesan
   (or an alternative vegetarian hard
   cheese)

1 teaspoon lemon juice

1 teaspoon grated lemon zest

salt and freshly ground black pepper

1 to 2 tablespoons gluten-free
   vegetable broth

Wild mushrooms lend a certain restaurant elegance to this pesto, which you can use on grilled meats or just on toast. You can buy gluten-free vegetable broth, but a lot of the ingredients I'm using here—carrots, parsley, kale stalks, mushrooms—can all make a good broth by themselves, just simmered for 20 minutes. Broccoli and cauliflower are also excellent.

1 Heat the oil in a pan and stir-fry the mushrooms over high heat for 2 to 3 minutes. Add the shallots and fry for another 2 to 3 minutes until the liquid has evaporated. Take out and let cool.

2 Add the fried mushrooms, parsley, and almonds to a food processor and blend until they form a pesto that is not too fine.

3 Fold in the Parmesan with the lemon juice and lemon zest and season with salt and pepper. Depending on the desired consistency, stir a little broth into the pesto.

See photo page 123

Carrot and Almond Spread with Dill

Per person: 488 calories, 12g protein, 43g fat, 9g carbohydrate, 12.5g fiber | Keto factor: 72

SERVES 1
Prep: 20 minutes

2 carrots, peeled and chopped
4 teaspoons butter
1–2 shallots, peeled and finely diced
2 tablespoons almond meal
2 tablespoons flaxseed meal
½ cup gluten-free vegetable broth
½ teaspoon grated lemon zest
1 to 2 sprinkles of lemon juice
1 to 2 pinches of cayenne pepper
salt and freshly ground black pepper
2 tablespoons full-fat cream cheese
2 tablespoons fresh or frozen dill

This spread goes with all the breads in this book and makes a delicious quick lunch. You can pack it into an airtight container and take to work with a couple of slices of bread for lunch on the go.

1 Put the carrots into a blender and crush to a rice-like consistency.

2 Heat the butter in a saucepan, add the shallots, and cook over medium heat until translucent.

3 Add the carrots and simmer for 6 to 7 minutes, stirring occasionally.

4 Sprinkle the almond and flaxseed meal over the top and mix in. Pour in half the broth and continue to cook until the carrots are tender. If needed, stir in the remaining broth.

5 Take off the heat and add the lemon zest, lemon juice, and cayenne pepper. Season with salt and pepper. Let the mixture cool down a bit, then mix in the cream cheese and dill and season again.

6 The dip should be kept chilled in the refrigerator and consumed within 1 to 2 days.

Tip
Try this as a tasty filling on the crepes (see page 118), rolled up into a wrap. This results in 787 calories, 25g protein, 68g fat, 11g carbohydrate, and 22g fiber per person (Keto factor: 78).

Kohlrabi Salad with Avocado & Lime Dressing

Per person: 409 calories, 8g protein, 36g fat, 12g carbohydrate, 14.5g fiber | Keto factor: 79

SERVES 1
Prep: 15 minutes

FOR THE SALAD
1 kohlrabi
1 small bunch fresh flat-leaf parsley,
    finely chopped
¼ cup unsweetened
    shredded coconut
1 teaspoon grated lime zest
1 to 2 pinches of red pepper flakes

FOR THE DRESSING
1 small avocado, coarsely chopped
1 small garlic clove, chopped
1 tablespoon lime juice
3½ tablespoons vegan gluten-free
    vegetable broth
salt and freshly ground black pepper

1 For the salad, peel the kohlrabi, remove the woody parts, cut into very fine strips on a julienne grater, and put into a bowl.

2 Mix half of the chopped parsley into the kohlrabi.

3 For the dressing, place the avocado and garlic with the lime juice and broth in a tall mixing bowl and purée with a hand blender. Season with salt and pepper. Drizzle the dressing over the kohlrabi strips and mix.

4 Roast the shredded coconut in a pan until golden. Mix with the remaining parsley, the lime zest, and the red pepper flakes and sprinkle over the salad.

Arugula & Avocado Salad with Oyster Mushrooms

Per person: 394 calories, 8g protein, 39g fat, 2.5g carbohydrate, 16g fiber | Keto factor: 89

SERVES 1
Prep: 15 minutes

2½ cups arugula
7 ounces oyster mushrooms
1 small avocado, cubed
salt and freshly ground black pepper
1 tablespoon peanut oil
1 tablespoon tamari (gluten-free
    soy sauce)
1 tablespoon lime juice
1 to 2 pinches of red pepper flakes

1 Line a bowl with the arugula.

2 Tear the mushroom caps into strips. Spread the avocado on the arugula and season with salt and pepper.

3 Heat the oil in a pan and stir-fry the mushrooms for 3 to 4 minutes over high heat. Deglaze with the tamari and continue frying until the liquid has evaporated.

4 Spread the mushrooms on the avocado cubes. Dissolve the residue in the pan with the lime juice and drizzle over the salad.

5 Sprinkle with the red pepper flakes.

Cauliflower Salad with Curry & Coconut Topping

Per person: 509 calories, 13g protein, 44g fat, 15g carbohydrate, 13.5g fiber | Keto factor: 85

SERVES 1
Prep: 15 minutes

FOR THE SALAD
1 teaspoon ground turmeric
salt and freshly ground black pepper
1 small head cauliflower
5 tablespoons full-fat cream cheese
1 tablespoon full-fat mayonnaise
1 teaspoon tamari (gluten-free
    soy sauce)
1 teaspoon curry powder
¼ cup cherry tomatoes, quartered
1 scallion, sliced
½ large bunch fresh flat-leaf parsley,
    coarsely chopped

FOR THE TOPPING
¼ cup unsweetened
    shredded coconut
½ teaspoon cumin seeds
¼ teaspoon red pepper flakes

You can use the leftover parsley, scallions, and tomato to make a broth with the water you use to simmer the cauliflower. Keto broth! Very handy to keep around the kitchen for other recipes.

1 Fill a saucepan with water, add the turmeric and a little salt to the water, and bring to a boil.

2 While the water is boiling, divide the cauliflower into equal bite-size florets. Add to the boiling water and cook for 5 to 6 minutes until al dente. Pour the cauliflower into a colander, rinse with cold water, and let drain.

3 Meanwhile, mix the cream cheese with the mayonnaise, tamari, curry powder, and a little salt and pepper in a bowl. Add the cauliflower and mix.

4 Mix in the tomatoes, scallion, and half of the parsley.

5 Roast the coconut and the cumin seeds in a pan until golden. Remove from the heat and stir in the red pepper flakes. Sprinkle the topping with the remaining parsley over the salad.

Tip
Try a variation: Replace half of the cauliflower with a small, diced avocado. Add the avocado to the sauce in the bowl. Proceed as specified in the recipe. This results in 708 calories, 12g protein, 67g fat, 13g carbohydrate, and 17g fiber per serving (Keto factor: 85).

Cabbage Coleslaw with Pecans

Per person: 541 calories, 11g protein, 49g fat, 11.5g carbohydrate, 13g fiber | Keto factor: 82

SERVES 1

Prep: 15 minutes

1 small piece of cabbage, such as pointed (hipsi/sweetheart) or napa, cut into fine strips

2½ teaspoons brown or golden flaxseed or 4 teaspoons flaxseed meal

1 small bunch fresh chives, cut into small rounds

1 large carrot, julienned

3½ tablespoons crème fraîche

4 teaspoons full-fat mayonnaise

1 teaspoon Dijon mustard

1 teaspoon tomato paste

1 teaspoon lemon juice

1 to 2 pinches of cayenne pepper

salt and freshly ground black pepper

¼ cup pecans

Like the cauliflower, the humble cabbage is budget-friendly and packs a lot of keto nutrition. This knocks non-keto coleslaw out of the game.

1 Salt and knead the cabbage vigorously for 1 minute until the cabbage becomes smoother.

2 Coarsely chop the flaxseed, if using, in a food processor. Mix the chives, cabbage, carrot, and flaxseed in a bowl.

3 Mix the crème fraîche with the mayonnaise, Dijon mustard, tomato paste, lemon juice, and cayenne pepper together and season with salt and pepper. Drizzle over the cabbage mixture and mix well.

4 Chop the pecans and sprinkle over the coleslaw.

Broccoli Macadamia Salad

Per person: 399 calories, 16g protein, 32g fat, 9.5g carbohydrate, 13g fiber | Keto factor: 72

SERVES 1
Prep: 10 minutes

1 large head broccoli, cut into florets
    and stalks
2 tablespoons tamari (gluten-free
    soy sauce)
1 teaspoon wheatgerm oil
1 teaspoon toasted sesame oil
½ bunch fresh flat-leaf parsley,
    stems and leaves chopped
2 tablespoons roasted sesame seeds
4 teaspoons brown or golden
    flaxseed
1 to 2 pinches of red pepper flakes
freshly ground black pepper
¼ cup macadamia nuts,
    coarsely chopped

I have used eight different spices to liven up this broccoli. And you can tell the difference from plain old florets with butter, or what we used to call them in school—trees!

1 Peel the broccoli stalks, if necessary. Grate both the broccoli florets and stalks coarsely on a grater and put into a bowl. Drizzle the tamari and both oils on top and mix.

2 Mix the parsley leaves and stems with the sesame seeds, flaxseed, and red pepper flakes and add to the salad. Season with pepper (salt is not necessary due to the soy sauce).

3 Sprinkle the macadamia nuts over the salad.

Tip
You can also use 2 teaspoons of wheatgerm oil instead of the combination of wheatgerm and sesame oils.

Zucchini Soup

Per person: 370 calories, 7g protein, 34g fat, 8g carbohydrate, 22g fiber | Keto factor: 83

SERVES 1
Prep: 15 minutes

2 teaspoons cold-pressed coconut oil
1–2 shallots, chopped
3½ ounces zucchini, diced into ½ to 5-inch squares
4 ounces black salsify (scorzonera) or artichoke hearts (from a jar)
½ teaspoon curry powder
¾ cup gluten-free vegetable broth
5 tablespoons heavy cream
1 to 2 pinches of cayenne pepper
pinch of freshly grated nutmeg
1 to 2 squeezes of lemon juice
salt and freshly ground black pepper
2 to 3 chives, cut into small rounds

1 Heat the coconut oil in a saucepan and sauté the shallots over medium heat until transparent. Add the zucchini and sauté for 1 minute. Add the salsify or artichoke hearts, sprinkle with the curry powder, stir, and add the broth.

2 Bring the mixture to a boil, cover, and simmer for about 4 minutes until the zucchini is just tender. Remove from the heat, pour in the cream, and purée with a hand blender. Stir in the cayenne pepper, nutmeg, and lemon juice, and season with salt and pepper.

3 Pour the soup into a deep plate or soup bowl and sprinkle the chives over it.

Note
3½ ounces of the black salsify already provide 17g fiber (artichoke hearts have less, at 4g fiber). Therefore, they can be combined well with low-fiber zucchini, which contains only 1g of fiber per 100g.

Vegetable & Potato Soup

Per person: 415 calories, 9 g protein, 34 g fat, 12.5 g carbohydrate, 17g fiber | Keto factor: 74

SERVES 1
Prep: 10 minutes

1 cup gluten-free vegetable broth
1 cup frozen vegetables or soup greens (mixture of carrot, celery, leek, onions, and herbs)
4 teaspoons potato fibers
½ cup heavy cream
1 teaspoon Dijon mustard
pinch of freshly grated nutmeg
salt and freshly ground black pepper
1 teaspoon chopped fresh parsley

1 Bring the vegetable broth to a boil in a pot, add the frozen vegetables or soup greens, bring to a boil again, and cook for 1 minute. Stir in the potato fibers and cook for another 3 to 4 minutes.

2 Stir in the cream, mustard, and nutmeg and season with salt and pepper. Pour the soup into a deep plate or soup bowl and sprinkle with the parsley.

Tip
Also try this hearty version: Cut a Viennese sausage into thin slices and heat it up in the soup. This results in 671 calories, 19g protein, 57g fat, 13g carbohydrate, and 17g fiber per person (Keto factor: 76).

Cauliflower Soup

Per person: 411 calories, 13g protein, 32g fat, 13g carbohydrate, 12.5g fiber | Keto factor: 70

SERVES 1

Prep: 20 minutes

1 tablespoon butter
1 to 2 shallots, diced
½ medium cauliflower,
    finely chopped
1 cup gluten-free vegetable broth
½ cup whole milk
2 tablespoons potato fibers
4 tablespoons full-fat cream cheese
1 teaspoon lemon juice
1 to 2 pinches of cayenne pepper
pinch of freshly grated nutmeg
salt and freshly ground black pepper
handful of alfalfa sprouts

Potato flour is gluten free and a great way to thicken sauces, gravies, and soups. It can also be used in baking. There is a variation you might find with other benefits from sweet potato flour. Worth experimenting.

1 Melt the butter in a saucepan and braise the shallots over medium heat, then add the cauliflower and sauté. Pour in the broth, bring to a boil, put the lid on, and simmer for 8 to 10 minutes.

2 Pour the milk into a saucepan and purée the cauliflower mixture with a hand blender. Add the potato fibers and mix again finely. Stir in the cream cheese.

3 Add the lemon juice, cayenne, and nutmeg, and season with salt and pepper. Pour the soup into a deep plate or soup bowl and sprinkle the sprouts over the top.

Celery Root Noodles in Cream Cheese Parmesan Sauce

Per person: 471 calories, 19g protein, 39g fat, 9g carbohydrate, 14g fiber | Keto factor: 75

SERVES 1
Prep: 20 minutes

1 tablespoon peanut oil
¼ celery root, cut into fine "noodles" with a spiralizer
⅓ leek from the firm white part, halved lengthwise and cut into strips
⅔ cup gluten-free vegetable broth
4 tablespoons full-fat cream cheese
1½ teaspoons inulin
½ cup freshly grated Parmesan (or an alternative vegetarian hard cheese)
1 to 2 pinches of cayenne pepper
pinch of freshly grated nutmeg
salt and freshly ground black pepper
1 bunch fresh flat-leaf parsley, chopped

One to surprise your guests or even yourself. It looks like pasta, only it's spriralized celery root—or what is known in classic French cooking as a remoulade. My version is keto friendly.

1 Heat the oil in a wok or pan and sauté the celery root over medium heat for 1 minute, without changing color. Add the leek and stir-fry for another minute.

2 Add the broth to the mixture, bring to a boil, put on the lid, and cook for 4 to 8 minutes until firm to the bite, depending on the "noodle" thickness.

3 Stir the cream cheese into the celery root mixture, then fold in the inulin and Parmesan. Season with cayenne pepper, nutmeg, and a little salt and pepper.

4 Fill a pasta plate or bowl with the celery root "pasta" and sprinkle with the parsley.

Spinach Leaves with High-Fiber Pesto & Egg

Per person: 570 calories, 28g protein, 46g fat, 5g carbohydrate, 14.5g fiber | Keto factor: 79

SERVES 1

Prep: 15 minutes

FOR THE PESTO

2 tablespoons golden flaxseed or
   3 tablespons flaxseed meal
⅓ bunch fresh basil, chopped
1 bunch fresh flat-leaf parsley,
   chopped
1 garlic clove, chopped
¼ cup slivered almonds
¼ cup freshly grated Parmesan
   (or an alternative vegetarian hard
   cheese)
1 tablespoon olive oil
4 to 6 teaspoons gluten-free
   vegetable broth
salt and freshly ground black pepper

FOR THE SPINACH AND EGG

1 teaspoon butter
1 large egg
salt and freshly ground black pepper
1½ cups frozen leaf spinach
1 pinch of freshly grated nutmeg

All the fiber here is in the pesto to compensate for the egg, which I have paired off in classic style with spinach, which is also full of carotenoids. Popeye was right!

1 Coarsely chop the flaxseed, if using, in a food processor. Add the herbs, garlic, and slivered almonds until a light mixture forms.

2 Put the mixture into a bowl, stir in the Parmesan and olive oil, and pour in the broth until a desired consistency is achieved. Season with salt and pepper.

3 Heat the butter in a small pan. Beat the egg and fry it over medium heat. Season with salt and pepper.

4 Squeeze and pour in the spinach. Season the spinach with nutmeg, a little salt, and pepper and put on a plate. Pour the pesto over the top and mix it in partially. Put the fried egg on top.

Tip

You can also combine the pesto with other vegetables, such as roasted asparagus or braised tomato slices. Diluted with more broth, it can also be used as a sauce or dressing. Allow 10 minutes for the pesto as preparation time. This results in 398 calories, 14 g protein, 35g fat, 3g carbohydrate, and 9g fiber per person (Keto factor: 79).

Zucchini with Macadamia & Arugula Sauce

Per person: 506 calories, 10g protein, 48g fat, 6.5g carbohydrate, 11.5g fiber | Keto factor: 83

SERVES 1

Prep: 10 minutes (without spread)

1 to 2 firm zucchini

1 serving of Macadamia Arugula Spread (see page 66)

4 tablespoons vegan, gluten-free vegetable broth

1 tablespoon cold-pressed coconut oil

salt and freshly ground black pepper

Over the week I build up my own secret stash of different sauces, dips, and pestos—this one we made earlier on page 66. With that on hand, you can make this dish in less than three minutes.

1 Cut the zucchini into "noodles" and dab them between paper towels.

2 Mix the macadamia arugula spread with the vegetable broth into a sauce. Heat the coconut oil in a wok and stir-fry the zucchini for 1 to 3 minutes, depending on the thickness.

3 Stir in the sauce and heat briefly; the zucchini should remain firm to the bite. Season with salt and pepper and serve immediately.

Tip

Try a variation: Place the same amount of small cauliflower or broccoli florets in the wok instead of the zucchini and fry in hot coconut oil. Then, pour in the vegetable broth, put the lid on, and cook until al dente. Finally, stir in the spread and season to taste. This results in 512 calories, 11g protein, 48g fat, 6.5g carbohydrate, and 15g fiber per person (Keto factor: 84) for the cauliflower or 520 calories, 12g protein, 48g fat, 7g carbohydrate, and 15.5g fiber per person (Keto factor: 83) for the broccoli.

Pan-Fried Vegetables & Pimientos

Per person: 543 calories, 7g protein, 52g fat, 12g carboyhdrate, 13g fiber | Keto factor: 85

SERVES 1

Prep: 15 minutes

3 scallions
1 tablespoon olive oil
10 green pimientos
¼ cup cherry tomatoes, quartered
1 small avocado, coarsely diced
1 teaspoon sherry vinegar
1 to 2 pinches of red pepper flakes
salt and freshly ground black pepper
¼ cup walnuts, coarsely chopped
1 small bunch fresh flat-leaf parsley,
    chopped

I love cooking in a pan. It's so easy, with very little mess, and there is always a sense of triumph when the smells fill the kitchen. You're building the flavors as you go.

1 Cut the scallions into small rounds, white and green parts cut separately. Heat the oil in a pan and fry the pimientos over medium heat for 3 minutes, turning frequently. Add the white scallion rings and fry for 1 minute.

2 Add the tomatoes and fry for another minute, turning frequently. Add the avocado and fry for 2 minutes. Stir in the sherry vinegar and red pepper flakes and season with salt and pepper.

3 Put the vegetable mixture on a serving plate and sprinkle with the walnuts, parsley, and green scallion rings. The dish tastes good either hot or lukewarm.

Asparagus with High-Fiber Topping

Per person: 518 calories, 22g protein, 41g fat, 12.5g carbohydrate, 13.5g fiber | Keto factor: 71

SERVES 1
Prep: 15 minutes

5 teaspoons olive oil
1 pound asparagus, peeled and cut
    into thirds
½ leek from the firm white part, cut
    lengthwise into strips
1 bunch fresh flat-leaf parsley, stems
    and leaves chopped separately
1 to 2 sprinkles of lemon juice
 salt and freshly ground
    black pepper
handful of Topping with Mixed
    Seeds (see page115)
2-inch piece of Parmesan (or
    an alternative vegetarian
    hard cheese)

When asparagus is in season there is always too much to go around, but this makes a great change from just butter or that old hotel cliché of a mashed hard-boiled egg. Out of season you could try this with purple sprouting broccoli instead.

1 Heat the oil in a pan and cook the thicker asparagus pieces over medium to high heat, stirring frequently, for 2 to 3 minutes. Add the remaining pieces of asparagus with the leek and parsley stems and cook for another 2 minutes.

2 Add the lemon juice and season with salt and pepper. Sprinkle the seed topping and parsley leaves over the asparagus mixture and partly mix in.

3 Put the vegetables on a plate and shave the Parmesan over the top with a vegetable peeler.

Fish Fillet with Mustard Sauce on Broccoli Purée

Per person: 584 calories, 32g protein, 46g fat, 10g carbohydrate, 12g fiber | Keto factor: 71

SERVES 1
Prep: 20 minutes

FOR THE PURÉE
½ head broccoli, stalks and florets
    peeled and cut separately
2 teaspoons flaxseed oil
salt and freshly ground black pepper

FOR THE FISH
4 teaspoons olive oil
1 to 2 shallots, finely chopped
½ cup gluten-free vegetable broth
1 tablespoon grainy mustard
3½ tablespoons full-fat
    cream cheese
1½ teaspoons inulin
1 teaspoon ground turmeric
salt and freshly ground black pepper
4½ ounces pollock or cod fillet,
    any bones removed

I'm using pollock here because it was inexpensive and unfashionable but still good—all fish to my mind is good as long as it is very fresh. The sauce, though, works well with other fish fillets, which are quick and easy to cook.

1 For the purée, bring some lightly salted water to a boil in a saucepan and insert a steaming basket—it should not touch the water. Put the broccoli florets and stalks into the steamer basket, put the lid on, and cook for 7 to 8 minutes.

2 Meanwhile, start the fish: heat 2 teaspoons of the olive oil in a saucepan and sauté the shallots over medium heat for about 2 to 3 minutes until transparent. Pour in the broth, stir in the mustard, cream cheese, and inulin, and simmer over low heat for 3 to 4 minutes. Stir in the turmeric and season with salt and pepper.

3 Heat the remaining 2 teaspoons olive oil in a pan. Lightly salt and fry the pollock fillet over medium heat on both sides for 1 to 2 minutes. Pour the sauce out of the saucepan into a serving bowl, switch off the stove, and finish cooking the fish gently for about 2 to 3 minutes.

4 Meanwhile, put the broccoli into a tall blender bowl and mash it coarsely with an immersion blender.

5 Stir in the flaxseed oil and season with salt and pepper. Put the broccoli purée on a plate and arrange the fillet with the sauce poured on top and alongside.

Herring with Herb Sour Cream & Broccoli

Per person: 569 calories, 29g protein, 45g fat, 11g carbohydrate, 11.5g fiber | Keto factor: 71

SERVES 1

Prep: 15 minutes

½ head broccoli, cut into florets
5 tablespoons sour cream
handful of fresh or frozen
    mixed herbs
½ teaspoon Dijon mustard
1½ teaspoons inulin
salt and freshly ground black pepper
4½ ounces herring fillets
    (from a jar)
1 scallion, cut into thin rings

A jar of herring is a good standby in the pantry for when you don't have much time to shop. After making a sauce for the fish with half the broccoli in the last recipe, I'm using the rest up here, just plain and simple and steamed.

1 Bring some salted water to a boil in a saucepan and insert a steaming basket—it should not touch the water. Put the broccoli florets into the steamer basket, put the lid on, and cook for 6 to 8 minutes until al-dente.

2 Mix the sour cream with the herbs, mustard, and inulin and season with salt and pepper. Lift out the steaming basket with the broccoli and let the steam evaporate a little.

3 Put the broccoli on a plate, arrange the herring with the herb sour cream on the side, and sprinkle the scallion rings over the top.

Cauliflower in a Fast Bolognese All'arrabbiata

Per person: 563 calories, 30g protein, 44g fat, 9g carbohydrate, 1 g fiber | Keto factor: 71

SERVES 1

Prep: 15 minutes

½ small head cauliflower, cut into
    ¾-inch florets
salt and freshly ground black pepper
4 teaspoons peanut oil
½ cup ground beef
1 to 2 shallots, diced
5 teaspoons tomato paste
¼ teaspoon dried thyme
¾ cup gluten-free meat or
    vegetable broth
2 tablespoons potato fibers
1 teaspoon sambal oelek (chili paste)

The keto classic—ground beef and cauliflower with a tomato-inspired sauce spiked with chili paste. The midweek TV dinner par excellence.

1 Bring some water to a boil in a saucepan and insert a steaming basket—it should not touch the water. Put the cauliflower florets into the steamer basket, put the lid on, and cook for 5 to 6 minutes. Remove, let evaporate, and sprinkle with salt.

2 Heat 2 teaspoons of the oil in a pan and sear the ground beef over high heat for 2 to 3 minutes, stirring, but do not cook through. Reduce the heat to medium and push the meat to the edge.

3 Heat the remaining 2 teaspoons of oil in the middle of the pan and sauté the shallots until transparent, then push them aside. Add the tomato paste and stir-fry for 1 minute, then mix well with the shallots and meat. Add the thyme and deglaze with the broth.

4 Stir in the potato fibers with the sambal oelek and season with salt and pepper. Fold in the cauliflower florets and briefly warm them up. Put the dish on a plate and serve.

Tip
You can replace the potato fibers with 1 tablespoon inulin. Then you can add ½ to ⅔ cup broth, because inulin binds with less liquid. This results in 556 calories, 29g protein, 44g fat, 9g carbohydrate, and 15.5g fiber per person (Keto factor: 71).

High-Fiber Meatballs with Buttered Veggies

Per person: 670 calories, 30g protein, 52g fat, 13g carbohydrate, 16g fiber | Keto factor: 70

SERVES 1
Prep: 20 minutes (without spread)

4 teaspoons butter
1 shallot, finely chopped
½ cup ground meat
2 teaspoons Dijon mustard
2 teaspoons tomato paste
salt and freshly ground black pepper
1 teaspoon psyllium fiber powder
1 tablespoon freshly crushed
    brown flaxseed
2 tablespoons almond meal
1 teaspoon canola oil
1¼ cups frozen peas and frozen
    carrots, mixed
2 sprigs fresh flat-leaf parsley,
    chopped

The advantage of ground meat over a chop or a steak is you can slip things into the mix to boost the keto nutrition. Here I'm going for the full high fives.

1 Heat 1 teaspoon of butter in a small pan and cook the shallot until translucent, then place in a bowl. Add the ground meat with the mustard and tomato paste and knead. Season with salt and pepper. Mix in the psyllium fiber powder, flaxseed, and almonds and form the mixture into two equal-size meatballs.

2 Heat the oil in the same pan and fry the meatballs slowly over medium heat for 10 minutes, turning frequently. Meanwhile, put the vegetables into a saucepan with 3 tablespoons of water and bring to a boil. Season with salt, put the lid on, and cook for 8 to 10 minutes. Drain and let evaporate a little.

3 Arrange the vegetables with the meatballs on a plate. Melt the remaining butter in flakes on the vegetables and sprinkle over the parsley.

Recipe finder

PHASE ONE: KETO BOOST

Morning Bowl with Strawberries, Avocado & Cottage Cheese	53
Morning Bowl with Chia & Coconut	53
Morning Bowl with Egg, Tomato & Avocado	54
Morning Bowl with Cucumber, Radish & Pistachio Pesto	57
Smoothie with Cucumber, Blueberries, Coconut Milk & Mint	58
Smoothie with Spinach, Avocado, Zucchini & Ginger	58
Keto High-Fiber Bread with Quark & Almonds	61
Keto High-Fiber Crispbread	62
Avocado, Pecan & Chive Spread	65
Sesame & Celery Root Spread	66
Macadamia Arugula Spread	66
High-Fiber Sandwich Bread	69
Sauerkraut, Mustard Mayonnaise & Pastrami Sandwich	70
Chile Mayonnaise, Lettuce & Egg Sandwich	70
Avocado, Wasabi & Smoked Salmon Sandwich	71
Ham Salad with Gherkins	73
Tomato, Avocado & Mozzarella Salad with Almond Pesto	73
Asparagus & Avocado Salad with Peanuts, Chile & Cilantro	74
Spicy Egg Salad	77
Parsnip & Coconut Soup with Curry	78
Spinach Soup with Parmesan	80
Radish "Fries" with Egg & Flax-Shallots	81
Mediterranean Celery Root with Feta Cheese, Olives & Pumpkin Seeds	82
Kale & Cheese Omelet	85
Mushroom Scallion Omelet	85
Cauliflower with a Parmesan Almond Crust	86
Salmon Fillet on Creamy Kale	89
Shrimp with Asparagus and Olive & Pistachio Topping	91
Chicken Broccoli Curry with Coconut Topping	93
Lamb Loin with Rosemary & Celery Purée	94
Carrot Noodles with Turkey Strips	97
Radish Noodles alla Carbonara	98

Recipe finder

PHASE TWO: STABILIZATION

Morning Bowl with Quark, Raspberries & Almonds	103
Morning Bowl with Blueberries & Crunchy Hemp Seeds	104
Morning Bowl with Avocado, Pumpkin Seed Pesto & Raspberries	105
Morning Bowl with Carrot, Avocado & Pumpkin Seeds	106
Kale Smoothie with Avocado, Cucumber & Coconut	108
Red Pepper Smoothie	108
Kale Smoothie with Cucumber & Peanut	109
Overnight Chia Muesli with Coconut & Hemp Seeds	112
Overnight Chia Muesli with Blueberries	112
Nutty Topping with Cacao Nibs	115
Topping with Mixed Seeds	115
Spicy Coconut Topping	115
Keto High-Fiber Nut Bread	116
Basic Crepes	118
Crepes with Spicy Cheese & Sprouts	118
Breakfast Crepes with Vanilla Yogurt & Berries	119
Crepes with Avocado & Carrot Filling	119
Mushroom Cream with Flaxseed & Pumpkin Seeds	122
Chanterelle Pesto	124
Carrot and Almond Spread with Dill	125
Kohlrabi Salad with Avocado & Lime Dressing	126
Arugula & Avocado Salad with Oyster Mushrooms	126
Cauliflower Salad with Curry & Coconut Topping	129
Cabbage Coleslaw with Pecans	130
Broccoli Macadamia Salad	133
Zucchini Soup	135
Vegetable & Potato Soup	135
Cauliflower Soup	136
Celery Root Noodles in Cream Cheese Parmesan Sauce	139
Spinach Leaves with High-Fiber Pesto & Egg	140
Zucchini with Macadamia & Arugula Sauce	143
Pan-Fried Vegetables & Pimientos	144
Asparagus with High-Fiber Topping	147
Fish Fillet with Mustard Sauce on Broccoli Purée	148
Herring with Herb Sour Cream & Broccoli	150
Cauliflower in a Fast Bolognese all'Arrabbiata	152
High-Fiber Meatballs with Buttered Veggies	155

General index

alcohol consumption 45–46
almonds 61, 73, 86, 103, 125
amino acids 29
antibiotics 23
arugula 66, 126, 143
asparagus 74, 91, 147
Atkins, Robert 17
avocados 27, 42, 53, 54, 58, 65, 71, 73, 74, 105, 106, 108, 119, 126

beef 30, 152
berries 15, 42, 119; see also blueberries; raspberries; strawberries
blood sugar levels 18, 29, 33
blueberries 58, 104, 112
bread, keto high-fiber 43, 61, 62, 69, 116
breads 27
broccoli 93, 133, 148, 150

cabbage 70, 130
cancers 10, 26, 30
carbohydrates 10–13, 16, 18, 24, 27, 32, 34
carrots 97, 106, 119, 125
cauliflower 86, 129, 136, 152
celery root 66, 82, 94, 139
cell growth 25
cheese 14, 30, 85, 118; see also cottage cheese; cream cheese; feta; mozzarella; Parmesan
chia seeds 53, 112
chicken 93
chile 70, 74
cholesterol levels 32
coconut 53, 58, 78, 93, 108, 112, 115, 129
coleslaw 130
cottage cheese 53
cream cheese 139
crepes 118–119
crispbread, keto high-fiber 62
cucumber 57, 58, 108, 109

dairy products 14; see also cheese; quark; yogurt
diabetes 18, 24, 34

eggs 14, 30, 43, 54, 70, 77, 81, 85, 140
energy 10, 25, 34

fasting 13
fat burning 10, 18
fats 14, 17, 18
  good and bad 24–27
fatty acids 24–26, 34
  Omega-3 27
  saturated 25
  short-chain fatty acids (SCFAs) 21
  unsaturated 25, 26
feta 82
fiber 11, 18, 20–23, 43; see also high-fiber diet
Firmicutes 23
fish 14, 25, 27, 30, 148; see also herring; salmon
flaxseed 81, 122
free radicals 11, 30
fruit 15, 42; see also specific varieties

gherkins 73
ginger 58
gut health 7, 11, 20–21

ham 73
hemp seeds 104, 112
herring 150
high-fiber diet 7, 16, 20–23, 40

immune system 10, 13, 30
inflammation 26, 27
insulin levels 7, 10, 11–13, 18, 29, 33, 34
inulin 43, 73, 77, 78, 118, 139, 148, 150

kale 85, 89, 108, 109
keto boost 7, 38, 51–98
keto factor 43
ketogenic diet
  benefits of 32–33
  defined 16
  effectiveness of 11
  how it works 18
  key ingredients 14–15, 42–43
  reasons for 34
  starting 47
ketones 11, 18, 33, 34, 39
ketosis 7, 11, 34, 39
kohlrabi 126

General index

lamb 30, 94
lipoproteins 32
low-carb diets 7, 10–13, 16
low-carb foods 14–15, 42–43
lycopene 30

macadamia nuts 66, 133, 143
macronutrients 24–30
meat 15, 29–30
  free-range 27
  see also specific types
meatballs 155
mental health 13
metabolic syndrome 33
metabolism 18
microbiome 13, 23, 32
micronutrients 24, 30
mindfulness when eating 44
mint 58
mozzarella 73
muesli 112
mushrooms 15, 85, 122, 124, 126

nutrients, macro and micro 24–30
nutritional supplements 26, 30
nuts 14, 27, 42; *see also* almonds; coconut;
  macadamia nuts; peanuts; pecans; pistachio nuts

obesity 7, 17, 26
oils 14, 26, 27, 42
olives 82, 91
Omega-3 fatty acids 27

Parmesan 80, 86, 98, 139
parsnips 78
pastrami 70
peanuts 74, 109
pecans 65, 130
peppers 108
pesto 57, 73, 105, 124, 140
physical activity 45
pimientos 144
pistachio nuts 57, 91
potatoes 135
protein 18, 24, 29–30

psyllium fiber powder 43, 61, 62, 69, 116, 155
pumpkin seeds 82, 105, 106, 122

quark 53, 61, 103

radishes 57, 81, 98
raspberries 103, 105
resveratrol 30

salads 73, 74, 77, 126, 129, 133
salmon 71, 89
saturated fats 24–26
sauerkraut 70
scallions 85
seafood 14, 91
seeds 14, 27, 42, 115; *see also* chia; flax; hemp;
  pumpkin; sesame
sesame seeds 66
shrimp 91
smoked salmon 71
smoothies 40, 58, 108, 109
snacking 44–45
sour cream 150
soy 30
spinach 58, 80, 140
sports, benefits for 34–35
strawberries 53

tofu 30
tomatoes 54, 73
toppings 91, 93, 115, 129, 147
trans fats 26
triglyceride 32–33
turkey 97

vegetables 15, 42, 135, 144; *see also specific
  varieties*
vitamins 26, 30

wasabi 71
weight loss 7, 10, 11, 18, 23, 33, 39

yogurt 14, 77, 119

zucchini 58, 135, 143

Tiller Press
An Imprint of Simon & Schuster, Inc.
1230 Avenue of the Americas
New York, NY 10020

First Tiller Press trade paperback edition in North America December 2020

English edition copyright © 2020 by Elwin Street Productions Limited
Translated from the German by Alison Tunley

Original edition published by Becker Joest Volk Verlag GmbH & Co. KG, Germany, in 2018
Text: Prof. Dr. med. Thomas Kurscheid
Recipes: Bettina Matthaei
Food styling: Stefan Mungenast
Photography: Hubertus Schüler, Benedikt Obermeier, Valentina Kurscheid, Shutterstock (pp 4, 19, 22, 27, 31, 40)

For information about special discounts for bulk purchases, please contact Simon & Schuster Special Sales at 1-866-506-1949 or business@simonandschuster.com.

The Simon & Schuster Speakers Bureau can bring authors to your live event. For more information or to book an event, contact the Simon & Schuster Speakers Bureau at 1-866-248-3049 or visit our website at www.simonspeakers.com.

Manufactured in China

10 9 8 7 6 5 4 3 2 1

Library of Congress Cataloging-in-Publication Data has been applied for.

ISBN 978-1-9821-5109-6